CW01303686

CLARE W. GRAVES
HIS LIFE AND HIS WORK

RAINER KRUMM & BENEDIKT PARSTORFER

GABAL global
English Editions by GABAL Publishing

iUniverse

CLARE W. GRAVES
HIS LIFE AND HIS WORK

Copyright © 2018 Rainer Krumm & Benedikt Parstorfer.

All rights reserved. No part of this book may be used or reproduced by any means, graphic, electronic, or mechanical, including photocopying, recording, taping or by any information storage retrieval system without the written permission of the author except in the case of brief quotations embodied in critical articles and reviews.

iUniverse books may be ordered through booksellers or by contacting:

iUniverse
1663 Liberty Drive
Bloomington, IN 47403
www.iuniverse.com
1-800-Authors (1-800-288-4677)

Because of the dynamic nature of the Internet, any web addresses or links contained in this book may have changed since publication and may no longer be valid. The views expressed in this work are solely those of the author and do not necessarily reflect the views of the publisher, and the publisher hereby disclaims any responsibility for them.

Any people depicted in stock imagery provided by Thinkstock are models, and such images are being used for illustrative purposes only.
Certain stock imagery © Thinkstock.

ISBN: 978-1-5320-3843-3 (sc)

Library of Congress Control Number: 2017918558

Print information available on the last page.

iUniverse rev. date: 01/24/2018

FOREWORD BY DON BECK

I first became aware of Professor Graves while teaching on the faculty of the University of North Texas, in Denton. My PhD study at the University of Oklahoma had focused on the work of Professor Muzafer Sherif, one of the founders of the discipline of Social Psychology. He had performed original work for decades in understanding how people align themselves into groups and alliances; how those human identities turn rigid as they become ego-involved, take life-time oaths, march in uniforms, and are drawn by the magic forces of Us vs. Them. Why do people almost anywhere hive off into belief systems, engage in a full range of actives that pull them apart even to the point of extreme polarization as they create deep divides and virtually destroy each other?

I did not find a more complete grasp of Why until I accidentally encountered the theory of Professor Graves. Now this will be a mindful definition: he called his framework the "emergent, cyclical, double-helix model of bio-psycho-social emergence."

I first met Graves 1975 at his home at his invitation. Graves was a tall, lean, intriguing figure of a man who loved Morgan, horses, sports of all kinds, Italian food and a lively challenge. He would sit at the back, eyes closed and lead bowed while I presented and illustrated HIS discovery. He was unmoved by fancy presentation slides and waited his turn to engage in lively interactions with the participants. Many would sit with minds in a daze, but with sparkles in their eyes. His health was not good at the time as bursts of sunlight blinded him. He carried his notes in a leather brown pouch and it never left his grasp.

Little did I know at the time that I had met a man with a powerful, insightful mind/brain that would someday join on the marquee with the likes of Freud, Skinner, Watson, Carl Rogers and others. He might well have broken the code to human survival. I was never the same myself.

After spending several years working with Prof. Graves in many different applications, even in several countries, it dawned on me that I was dealing with both a unique human being as well as a scholar that were truly special, almost one of a kind. The way he constructed his defining theory; the very cautious and patient way he formed it over several years, and even the manner in which he drew criticism from different viewing points that were threatened by it, I began to see it as Humanity's Master Code. Very much like a Master Key that unlocks many different situations and equations, it has the flexibility to deal with a myriad of choice-making options. I use that tribute carefully.

When I first encountered him I was analyzing 42 different systemic models from many different disciplines. None of the other 41 cause-effect packages could compare to his work, both in its complexity of understanding as well as its simplicity of use. The core of what he "discovered" was reflecting an understanding of how various variables hang together to resolve a specific set of problems. When a certain fusion becomes appropriate, the synergy between life conditions/challenges, and appropriate and functional solutions become obvious.

This was the primary reason I was able to enter South Africa at the peak of Apartheid and be heard, but eventually be in a position to assist in ways to dismantle it from the inside.

My work with Nelson Mandela is an example. If you have seen the movie INVICTUS you might get my point. I used sport — the Springbok rugby side in the 1995 World Cup to model how to use sport to create national unity; see my book The Crucible: Forging South Africa's Future.

During his retirement days, Pat and I sought to share with him our common interests and world events. He was a huge NFL football fan and never missed a hockey game played by students at Union College. He truly enjoyed the day I took to him to a practice session of the New Orleans Saints at the Super Bowl in New Orleans.

I continue to feel as alive as I looked back on the fence with Graves who is/was something of the "Godfather of the global Spiral dynamics theory and movement." While I do not claim to be the keeper of the orthodoxy, I have attempted to keep his thoughts and understanding of human dynamics as pristine as I could.

This book, an outstanding work by co-authors Rainer Krumm and Benedikt Parstorfer, is an important contribution to preserve, spread and further adapt Graves' work.

Together with my co-authors Teddy Hebo Larsen, Sergey Solonin, Rica Viljoen and Thomas Johns, I'm continuing the movement with the book *"Spiral Dynamics in Action: Humanity's Master Code"*, which will be focused on action over theory.

Don Edward Beck, PhD

drBeck@spiraldylnamics.net

Clare W. Graves with Don Beck

INTRODUCTION BY PROF. DR. THOMAS GINTER

The number of books dealing with the topic of "development and success" has grown epidemically in recent years. *"How do I do this?"* or *"How do I do that?"* are usually the fundamental issues with which these self-proclaimed miracle workers or *"downfall accelerators"* (to speak with Peter Sloterdijk) are concerned. The practical benefits of the *formulas for success, principles and methods* contained therein unfortunately all too often tend to be zero; the dynamics and complexities of our world are not so easily domesticated. This is all the more regrettable, but we now require a clear orientation that helps us to understand the conditions in an organizational, social and societal context.

The work of Clare W. Graves undoubtedly provides the basis for a deeper understanding of the world and of human actors. His complex yet unified theory construction provides a valued reference framework. Based on many years of research (instead of intuitions driven by zeitgeist), Graves developed the *"emerging, cyclical double helix model of biopsychosocial systems"*. At the time, the importance of this was only recognized by a small group of researchers. Graves was driven by the question: *"What exactly constitutes a mentally healthy individual?"* From there, he developed a system that retraced both phylogenetic and ontogenetic human development.

Graves received additional attention when his students Don Beck and Christopher Cowan reworked his theory construction. Through their book, *"Spiral Dynamics"* as well as the integral (Community by Ken Wilber, the aggregated work of Graves reached the 21st century. The editors of the current work *Rainer Krumm*, who as co-author of the German book *"Unternehmen verstehen, gestalten, verändern"* (Understanding, shaping, and changing enterprises) as well as *Benedikt Parstorfer*, who as a representative of the next generation adapted and updated the research of Graves, continue in this tradition. This book, *"Clare W. Graves: His life and his work"* takes the reader back to the beginnings and thus basics of Gravesian theory construction, which is a journey full of surprises and epiphanies.

Prof. Dr. Thomas Ginter

www.iwm-business.de

PREFACE OF THE AUTHORS

Today, a great deal of what is known as Spiral Dynamics[1] or 9 Levels of Value Systems [2] or the *integral theory* originated from Graves' double-helix model.

From our own experience in coaching and advising companies from different sectors and disciplines, we are aware of the strength and developmental potential of Graves' work. The objective of this book is to disseminate knowledge about Graves and his extensive work and to comprehensibly trace the development of his theory.

The importance of Graves' work has not yet been fully realized. However, in an increasingly complex world, we need models that can capture this complexity and provide a better understanding of the changes and challenges we face. The analysis of our own value systems, thoughts and actions helps us to raise the awareness of how we act, as individuals and within systems, and to thereby create the basis for targeted development.

Our claim to the work with Gravesian knowledge is simple: it should make a positive difference and be of high quality. This requires a thorough understanding of the original work. This book provides a summary of his work – "A theory that explains everything" - as it has been frequently called. We hope that this book will contribute to a deeper understanding and to making Graves' original work accessible to a broader audience.

Rainer Krumm & Benedikt Parstorfer

www.9levels.com

---

[1] SPIRAL DYNAMICS® is a registered trademark owned by NVCC
[2] 9 Levels Of Value Systems is a registered trademarks of 9 Levels Institute for value systems GmbH & Co. KG

CONTENTS

Foreword by Don Beck v
Introduction by Prof. Dr. Thomas Ginter ix
Preface of the Authors xi
List of Illustrations xvii

Introduction - "The Theory that Explains Everything" 1

Graves in Brief – Summary of an Interview 3

Clare W. Graves – the person 9
    Tabular Overview 17

The Development Of His Theory 19
    Motivation and Beginnings: "So Who Is Right?" 19
    Fundamental Questions: What exactly constitutes a
        Psychologically sound Individual? 19
    Data Collection 21
    Questions for Further Study 22
    Data Processing 23
    Continuing Research 25
    Let the data talk 26
    Conceptualization 32
    Cyclical 33
    Neurological systems 33
    Movement through the systems/levels 34
    Psychopathology 34
    Additional research methods 35
    Graves and Maslow 36

Chronological Representation of His Work and Lectures 38

Summary of the articles 43
  Master's thesis: Individual Differences in Irritability in the
     Male Rat (1943) 45
  Doctoral Thesis: A Study of the Genesis and Dynamics of
     Psychopathic Personality as Revealed by Combining the
     Clinical Case History and Experimental Approaches (1945) ... 47
  An Emergent Theory of Ethical Behavior – Based Upon an
     Epigenetic Model (1959) 50
  On the theory of ethical behavior (1961) 50
  The Implications to Management of Systems-Ethical Theory
     (1962) 52
  Levels of Human Existence and their Relation to Value
     Analysis and Engineering (1964–65) 53
  Value Systems and their Relation to Managerial Controls and
     Organizational Viability (1965) 55
  With Huntley and Labier: Personality Structure and Perceptual
     Readiness: an Investigation of their Relationship to
     Hypothesized Levels of Human Existence (1965) 57
  Deterioration of Work Standards (1966) 59
  With Madden, H.T. and Madden, L.P.: The Congruent
     Management Strategy (1970) 63
  The Levels of Human Existence and their Relation to Welfare
     Problems (1970) 75
  How Should Who Lead Whom To Do What? (1971–72) 76
  Levels of Existence Related to Learning Systems (1971) 78
  Human Nature Prepares for a Momentous Leap (1974) 81
  Summary Statement: The Emergent, Cyclical, Double-Helix
     Model of the Adult Human Biopsychosocial Systems (1981)... 86

Outlook 93
About the Authors 95
  Rainer Krumm 95
  Benedikt Parstorfer 96

Bibliography 97
    Graves' works – books, articles, and lectures 97
    Additional literature 98
    Film documents 99
    Audio documents 99
    Internet Sources 99

List of Sources for Figures 101

LIST OF ILLUSTRATONS

Figure 1: Portrait of Clare W. Graves... 9
Figure 2: The Union College campus in 1950. 10
Figure 3: Graves' most important career posts 11
Figure 4: Title page of his 1943 Master's thesis...................................... 12
Figure 5, above and below: Excerpt from the announcement of
    the Western Reserve University for Master of Arts 13
Figure 6: Title page of the doctoral thesis of Clare W. Graves 14
Figure 7: Autonomy... 27
Figure 8: Intelligence... 27
Figure 9: Authoritative attitude 28
Figure 10: Achieving new concepts 28
Figure 11: Creating innovations... 29
Figure 12: Self-control... 29
Figure 13: Belonging.. 30
Figure 14: Aggression 31
Figure 15: Independence 31
Figure 16: Title page of his 1943 Master's thesis.................................... 45
Figure 17: Title page of the doctoral thesis of Clare W. Graves 47

INTRODUCTION - "THE THEORY THAT EXPLAINS EVERYTHING"

In a 1967 article, Canadian journalist Nicholas Steed dubbed the works of Clare W. Graves as "the theory that explains everything". Graves did indeed succeed in developing a complex and comprehensive theory construction that is valuable and useful in many areas of human existence. Upon the first reading, the final name that Graves gave his work appears unwieldy:

"The emergent, cyclical, double-helix model of the adult human biopsychosocial systems development"

What this all means will be clarified in the following pages. With respect to the name of the model, he smugly told the audience at a lecture: *"I'm sorry, but that's what it is!"*

This book should enable experts on the theory or the modern forms of use such as SPIRAL DYNAMICS® and 9 LEVELS® to further immerse themselves and better understand the origins. For others with little or no knowledge of the theory, it can serve as both an introduction and a deeper dive into his work. We will begin with a summary of Graves' work, starting with his Master's and doctoral theses and continuing to his last articles.

During his lifetime, Graves' theory and work received little attention. However, various disciplines, ranging from psychology to pedagogy to business management, and their practical applications rely on it.

Don Beck and Christopher Cowan in particular have ensured that his work will not go unforgotten. They diligently documented his work, thus recording his knowledge. In 1974, Beck read "Futurist" and was impressed. He was a professor at Northern Texas University and flew to New York to meet Graves. After two days of dialogues, it was clear to Beck that he wanted to spend at least 10 years recording Graves' knowledge, as the latter's health was deteriorating.

Graves himself had never completely published his works in the form of a book. "Spiral Dynamics[3]" (1996) by Beck and Cowan was thus all the more important. They used a simplified and popularized model in management and leadership. It was only in 2005 that Christopher Cowan and Natasha Todorovic completed the works of Graves in a book entitled "The Never Ending Quest".

Thanks to William Lee, numerous texts and information are available under *www.clarewgraves.com*. Lee himself was a teacher of psychology in Virginia and met Graves at a seminar in Washington D.C. He also published several of Graves' writings in "Levels of Human Existence" (2002). Along with Cowan, Lee is one of the most important executors. Both passed away in 2015.

Graves had quite a large collection of data, which he kept in a horse stable on his property. However, following a heart attack and a stroke, he destroyed many of these documents. This is now decomposing in a landfill in New York.

This book was therefore created in order to provide the interested reader with intensive access to Graves and his works. It aims to describe Graves' life and trace the origins of his work in historical steps. Numerous graphics, which resemble the original depictions, additionally illustrate the evolutionary steps of his theory.

---

[3] SPIRAL DYNAMICS® is a registered trademark owned by NVCC

GRAVES IN BRIEF – SUMMARY OF AN INTERVIEW

One of the few film documents of Graves lends itself well to provide an initial impression of his intention, creativity and theory construction. Cliff Macintosh from the Quetico Centre interviewed Prof. Graves. The interview is probably from 1974, the year in which Graves also held a seminar there.

Macintosh and Graves sit comfortably on swiveling chairs. Between them is a small table with cups. On the wall of the room, which is reminiscent of a basement workshop, several flip charts are hung. The atmosphere is relaxed and casual.

When asked why he developed his theory, Graves answers that he wanted to understand the chaos in which humans exist and to develop a framework in which one could effectively deal with the problems of humans. Questioning the behavior of children, managers, or organizations always resulted in diverse and often contradictory answers. Graves wanted to find a way to study these conflicts and discrepancies.

The name ECLET (Emergent Cyclical Levels of Existence Theory) stems from Graves' research. Human psychology is emerging in terms of never-ending change. For Graves, there is no such thing as <u>the</u> adult human or <u>the</u> society. Instead, there are various constellations of problems that must be dealt with and coping mechanisms with which to do so.

On one hand, we attempt to cope with the external world in order to survive. However, if we focus on our inner world, we try to make peace with it. This shift between the external and internal accounts for the cyclical part of the model. By solving a set of problems, a new one is created.

Graves considers two psychological questions to be particularly interesting:

(1) Why do we have such a large brain?

(2) Why is it divided into two hemispheres?

For the purposes of his theory, he answers the first question by stating that we have another form of survival potential that we can develop to higher existential levels if the problems become more complex.

He explains the division into two hemispheres using the cyclical aspect. For the odd systems (beige 1, red 3, orange 5 and yellow 7), the left hemisphere is dominant and for the even systems (purple 2, blue 4, green 6) the right hemisphere is. Contrary to what many assume, the brain does not function like other organs that reach a certain level of maturity and remain there. Instead, it changes infinitely and has the capacity to always create new levels. The process activates parts of the brain that have never been active before.

Looking at one individual, the central question is how to solve his or her problems. Individuals are not a pure type. Instead, components of personality remain at one level while other components have already proceeded. However, one system will always dominate.

According to Graves, one possibility of gaining access is to ask individuals for their opinions on certain topics. For example, what does an individual at the blue level (4, D-Q) think about abortion compared to an individual at the orange level (5, E-R)? The same applies for styles of management. Job enrichment is an excellent motivation for individuals at the orange level (5, E-R), while the opposite is true for individuals at the blue level (4, D-Q). According to Graves, management at the yellow level (7, A'-N') would be different. The organization would seek to hire people from certain levels for certain positions in the enterprise. This type of management would only be possible at the yellow level (seven, A'-N'). All of the previous levels would be convinced that there is only one particular way of doing things. The same rules apply for all parts of the organization e.g. in schools for all grades.

For Graves, a liberal upbringing would be a fine thing if the world were a friendlier place. Such an upbringing does not prepare one for the tough aspects of life. Graves argues for a different approach to childcare: during the time in which a particular system develops, parents should be lax and give the child the possibility to explore this new set of possibilities that arise from within. Some time should be given for stabilization in order to awaken it and confront the difficult aspects of life. This would be particularly difficult for individuals at the green level (6, F-S). With the knowledge that we have about the levels of human existence, we could theoretically raise our children in such a manner that would continue to develop to a particular level. However, parents should be aware of the advantages and disadvantages of the individual levels.

In one example, potential conflicts between different levels become evident. If a woman at the green level (6, F-S) married a man at the orange level (5, E-R), this could lead to a rather miserable existence if they each observe the world from the perspective of their respective levels. If the man believes that ambition and reaching one's goals are more important than existence and shared experiences, his wife could experience difficulties in understanding this. However, if both of them are open and willing to learn, they can understand each other.

Managers should ideally be a level or step ahead of their employees. However, this is only the case if they are familiar with the suitable management principles and can apply them. Otherwise, problems will arise. For example, employees at the red level (3, C-P) cannot be led via reward and punishment because the system for this is not activated. In this case, this type of management is counterproductive.

When asked if there were individuals in the US who were at the beige (1, A-N) and purple levels (2, B-O), Graves answers affirmatively. The beige level (1, A-N) includes demented, severely pathological, senile, and mentally severely impaired individuals. According to Graves, individuals at the purple level (2, B-O) can be found in several reservations near Montreal and in the area between Little Rock and central Pennsylvania.

Cliff Macintosh asks whether fighting poverty in the form of social help is not doomed to failure from the onset. Graves agrees with him. According to him, individuals who are predominantly at the purple level (2, B-O) have a very different understanding of space and time compared to the initiators of such projects. They know their own block but have no perception of the city. They live in the "here and now" and do not plan ahead. However, in order to receive meal vouchers, they must be in a certain place at a certain time. Graves is convinced that this cannot work because of different concepts and will ultimately fail. However, organizations that react at the blue level (4, D-Q) do not understand this difference and would continue to offer programs according to this pattern.

How might an organization that primarily manages at the yellow level (7, A´-N´) look like? Graves assumes that such an organization would work in a problem-oriented manner instead of a process-oriented one. The management of operative processes loses importance and problems are dealt with as they arise. The focus here is on producing and offering things that are important for the advancement of humanity and contribute something positive to co-existence and not simply everything that can be sold.

What would the development activity in such an organization look like? Graves first had to clarify whether (1) the individuals were open or closed and (2) the jobs in the organization were changeable or not. Some work can only be performed in a single way in order to achieve the desired result. If the individuals are closed and the jobs are unchangeable, management should determine the appropriate management system with the appropriate remuneration system and selection process corresponding to the level of the respective area. In this context, progress refers to increasing managerial knowledge for this static system in order to be able to lead it in a better way. However, an organization that changes poses a completely different challenge – just like the individuals that work within it. This entails individuals to be open and to choose whom they would like to work with. If you have open individuals though, organizational development means to establish congruence between management, management processes, the users of these processes and the individuals in the production and customer service areas.

Graves criticizes the traditional concepts for team development because they don't consider whether or not a certain training makes sense for certain people. For example, team training would not benefit the orange level (5, E-R) because the participants would use the knowledge to their own advantage rather than for the community.

He cites a study of different types of organizational developers. According to this, there are three: (1) those fixated on human relations, (2) those with pre-determined success strategies who manipulate the organization until they are implemented, and (3) those with a systemic management approach. The third type of advisor answers the question of where to find the organization's problem with "How would I know? I just got here."

For Graves, there is no reason whatsoever for an end of change. For him, this is a never-ending process; we are a part of nature and nature is a process of never-ending change.

Graves refers to the physicist and Nobel laureate Werner Heisenberg and states that for him, things are simultaneously absolute and relative. Paradoxical thinking and ambiguities are consistent for him because they make sense if they are considered in a wider context.

When asked how he would classify himself, Graves answered that it strongly depended on the topic. However, he often thinks in a blue (4, D-Q) manner. Any theory is described from the level of the author; for this, one tends to need the yellow level (7, A'-N').

After nine years of scientific research, Graves attempted to adequately describe the results with existing theories: he found this process to be terrible because none of them really were a good fit. This made him realize something else. It is not a question of who is right; everybody was right. After two years of trying to find a suitable approach, he started accepting this.

When Graves began to collect his first raw data in 1952, approximately 34% of the subjects were at the blue level (4, D-Q) and 6% were at the yellow level (7, A'-N'). By 1969, when he collected the final data, the ratio had nearly inverted. There was to be a great change as soon as the generation of college students from 1969 assumed positions in middle and upper management. By the Orwellian year of 1984, Graves expected a development of management at the yellow level (7, A'- N'), whereby institutional life would take on a new form.

CLARE W. GRAVES – THE PERSON

"What constitutes a healthy adult?" – This simple, yet difficult-to-answer question led Graves to many years of research on his model of developmental psychology. During his lifetime, he was certainly not aware of the impact, importance and influence that his work would have.

Figure 1: Portrait of Clare W. Graves

Clare Wray Graves was born on December 21, 1914 in New Richmond, Indiana. Unfortunately, little is known about his childhood home and the circumstances in which he grew up. This would have been interesting to know because he always stressed how living conditions influenced human development.

New Richmond, which is approximately 60 miles northwest of Indianapolis, has less than 500 inhabitants and is situated in a predominantly agricultural region.

In 1940, he received a Bachelor of Arts in mathematics and sciences from Union College, which is a private university in Schenectady, New York. Today, Union College has an excellent reputation. Despite its small size, it ranked 26th in Forbes Top Colleges in 2009. Founded in 1795, shortly after American independence, Union College was among the first institutions to offer a university education.

Figure 2: The Union College campus in 1950.

It has one of the oldest and most remarkable campuses in the US, which was designed by French architect Joseph Ramée, who resided in the US between 1812 and 1816.

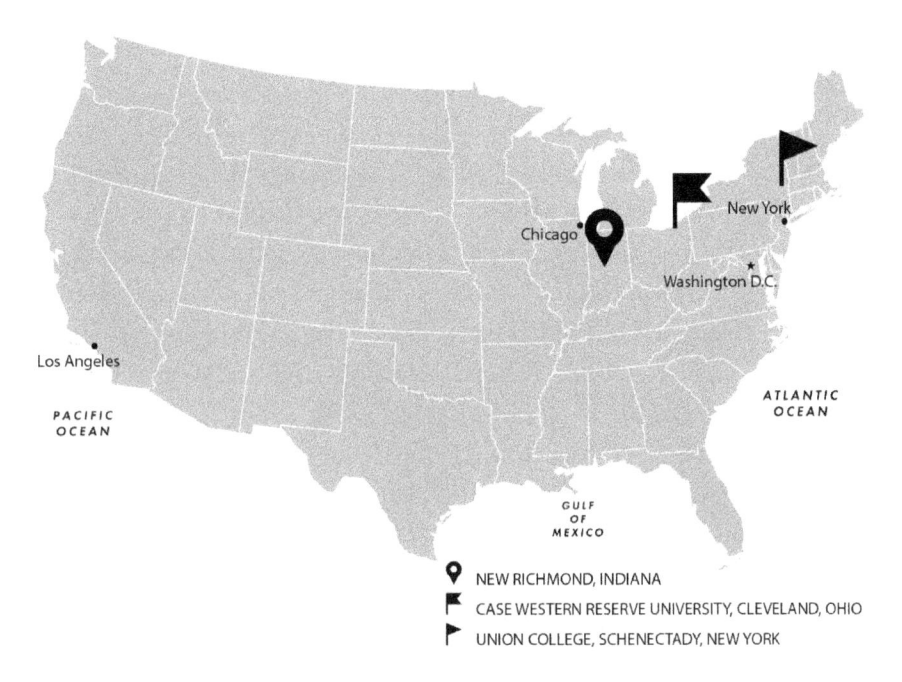

Figure 3: Graves' most important career posts

Schenectady is a city in Schenectady County in New York State. It is also the county seat. The city has been chiefly industrial since the 19th century. It is also known as the "Electric City" in honor of the company General Electric, which has been situated there since 1974. The city lies on the Mohawk River close to the junction with the Hudson River, which is approximately 140 miles north of New York City. It is roughly equidistant from the Atlantic to the southeast and Lake Erie to the west.

After completing his Bachelor's degree, Graves received a Master of Arts in psychology from Western Reserve University. In 1826, Western Reserve University was established in Hudson Ohio, which is approximately 26 miles from Cleveland. The university was later relocated to Cleveland as this city experienced substantial growth. The university is currently called Case Western Reserve University.

Graves completed his studies on 10 February 1943. His Master's thesis was entitled "Individual differences in irritability in the male rat". This comprised 41 typed pages and 18 references. He was supervised by Calvin S. Hall to whom he dedicated his work.

> ***Digression:*** Calvin Springer Hall (* 18 January 1909 in Seattle, Washington; † 4 April 1985 in Santa Cruz, California) was a US psychoanalyst and dream analyst. Hall first completed his studies in psychology in Washington under the renowned behaviorist, Edwin Guthrie. Because he refused a mandatory ROTC (Reserve Officers' Training Corps) course, he had to transfer to the University of California in Berkeley where he received his first degree in 1930 under the supervision of behaviorist Edward Tolman. After studying under Tolman and Robert Tryon, he received his doctorate in 1933. Until then, Hall had mainly dealt with behavioral experiments in rats. He was able to prove that – starting with the same genetic material – different circumstances could lead to different behavioral habits and learning abilities. From 1935 to 1975, Hall was one of the most creative psychologists in the US. Hall predominately taught at Case Western Reserve University (Cleveland, Ohio).

Figure 4: Title page of his 1943 Master's thesis

Clare W. Graves

WESTERN RESERVE UNIVERSITY

ANNUAL
COMMENCEMENT CONVOCATION

CLEVELAND
JUNE NINTH
NINETEEN FORTY THREE

Figure 5, above and below: Excerpt from the announcement of the Western Reserve University for Master of Arts

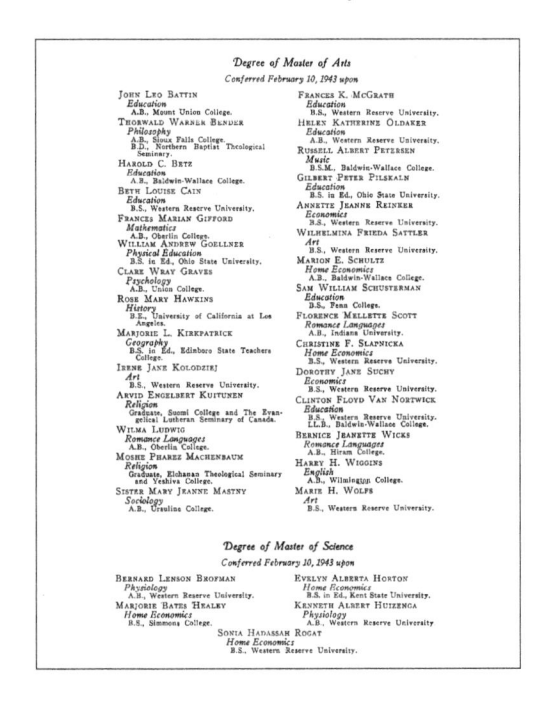

Degree of Master of Arts
Conferred February 10, 1943 upon

JOHN LEO BATTIN
Education
A.B., Mount Union College.
THORWALD WARNER BENDER
Philosophy
A.B., Sioux Falls College.
B.D., Northern Baptist Theological Seminary.
HAROLD C. BETZ
Education
A.B., Baldwin-Wallace College.
BETH LOUISE CAIN
Education
B.S., Western Reserve University.
FRANCES MARIAN GIFFORD
Mathematics
A.B., Oberlin College.
WILLIAM ANDREW GOELLNER
Physical Education
B.S. in Ed., Ohio State University.
CLARE WRAY GRAVES
Psychology
A.B., Union College.
ROSE MARY HAWKINS
History
B.S., University of California at Los Angeles.
MARJORIE L. KIRKPATRICK
Geography
B.S. in Ed., Edinboro State Teachers College.
IRENE JANE KOLODZIEJ
Art
B.S., Western Reserve University.
ARVID ENGELBERT KUITUNEN
Religion
Graduate, Suomi College and The Evangelical Lutheran Seminary of Canada.
WILMA LUDWIG
Romance Languages
A.B., Oberlin College.
MOSHE PHAREZ MACHENBAUM
Religion
Graduate, Elchanan Theological Seminary and Yeshiva College.
SISTER MARY JEANNE MASTNY
Sociology
A.B., Ursuline College.

FRANCES K. MCGRATH
Education
B.S., Western Reserve University.
HELEN KATHERINE OLDAKER
Education
A.B., Western Reserve University.
RUSSELL ALBERT PETERSEN
Music
B.S.M., Baldwin-Wallace College.
GILBERT PETER PILSKALN
Education
B.S. in Ed., Ohio State University.
ANNETTE JEANNE REINER
Economics
B.S., Western Reserve University.
WILHELMINA FRIEDA SATTLER
Art
B.S., Western Reserve University.
MARION E. SCHULTZ
Home Economics
A.B., Baldwin-Wallace College.
SAM WILLIAM SCHUSTERMAN
Education
B.S., Penn College.
FLORENCE MELLETTE SCOTT
Romance Languages
A.B., Indiana University.
CHRISTINE F. SLAPNICKA
Home Economics
B.S., Western Reserve University.
DOROTHY JANE SUCHY
Economics
B.S., Western Reserve University.
CLINTON FLOYD VAN NORTWICK
Education
B.S., Western Reserve University.
LL.B., Baldwin-Wallace College.
BERNICE JEANNETTE WICKS
Romance Languages
A.B., Hiram College.
HARRY H. WIGGINS
English
A.B., Wilmington College.
MARIE H. WOLPE
Art
B.S., Western Reserve University.

Degree of Master of Science
Conferred February 10, 1943 upon

BERNARD LENSON BROFMAN
Physiology
B.S., Western Reserve University.
MARJORIE BATES HEALEY
Home Economics
B.S., Simmons College.

EVELYN ALBERTA HORTON
Home Economics
B.S. in Ed., Kent State University.
KENNETH ALBERT HUIZENGA
Physiology
A.B., Western Reserve University.

SONIA HADASSAH ROGAT
Home Economics
B.S., Western Reserve University.

His doctoral thesis was entitled "A study of the genesis and dynamics of psychopathic personality as revealed by combining the clinical case history and experimental approaches". Like his Master's thesis at Western Reserve University (working under Calvin S. Hall), he submitted his doctoral thesis to the department of psychology.

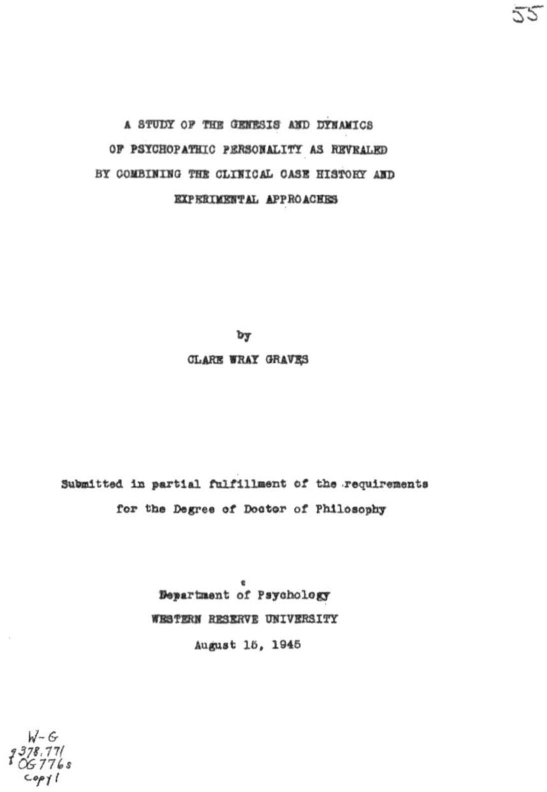

55

A STUDY OF THE GENESIS AND DYNAMICS
OF PSYCHOPATHIC PERSONALITY AS REVEALED
BY COMBINING THE CLINICAL CASE HISTORY AND
EXPERIMENTAL APPROACHES

by

CLARE WRAY GRAVES

Submitted in partial fulfillment of the requirements
for the Degree of Doctor of Philosophy

Department of Psychology
WESTERN RESERVE UNIVERSITY
August 15, 1945

Figure 6: Title page of the doctoral thesis of Clare W. Graves

Already back then, Graves was characterized by the fact that he thoroughly investigated topics and sources and also questioned and challenged established scientific information.

After several teaching assignments and a position as clinical psychologist in a rehabilitation center, in 1956, Graves returned to Union College as a professor of psychology. He taught and researched there until his retirement in 1978.

Graves felt at home in many professional areas. In many respects, he pursued a typical academic career. During his Master's studies at the Western Reserve University, he worked as a scientist and technical assistant. He then became an assistant professor and later a full professor at Union College (1958), where he taught until 1978.

In addition to his academic career, Graves also worked as a criminal psychologist in Cuyahoga County, Ohio. Furthermore, he was also employed as a clinical psychologist at the Cleveland Rehabilitation Centre between 1943 and 1946.

Alongside his teaching activities, Graves served as an advisor for clinical facilities as well as industry and economy. His clients included Dresser Industries, Apex Vacuum, ALCOA, GM, and New York Bell System. In the clinical field, he supervised youth courts, social services, prisons, rehabilitation centers, hospitals and health departments. The versatility of his practical work experience provided a sound basis for his university research on personality theory.

Graves was a member of respected organizations such as the American Psychological Association, the American Association of University Professors and the American Association for the Advancement of Science.

With the publication of his article "The Deterioration of Work Standards", his research was featured in the Harvard Business Review (1966). Graves, who had been unknown up until then, subsequently received a great deal of demand for his article. This was the most requested article in the history of the Harvard Business Review. According to one anecdote, Graves had one of his students to thank for the publication of his article. The student occasionally performed minor plumbing tasks for Graves. He saw the article in Graves' home and questioned him about it. Graves replied that he had written the article for the Harvard Business Review and that the editors rejected it. The student contacted the editors and expressed his outrage at how such a remarkable individual and article could go unnoticed. As a result, Graves' article was ultimately published.

He was married with Marian Graves (née Huff). They had two children, Susan and Robert. Graves suffered five strokes. On 3 January 1986, at the age of 71, he died in Rexford, New York.

Up until his death, he worked on his book, which aimed to summarize his theory and the results of his research. The working title was "Up the Existential Staircase". This book remained as an unpublished fragment. However, it was later assembled, reworked and published by Christopher C. Cowan and Natasha Todorovic under the title "The Never Ending Quest."

There is only limited information about Graves. He himself was surprised by the interest in his theory. He had retreated into a quiet and unassuming university life.

Looking at the video footage of Graves, one can see a quiet, intellectual man who did not long for fame but was motivated to obtain a deeper understanding of human development.

Frank "Ben" Swan, who graduated from Union College in 1950, remembers playing golf on the college team and that Graves had been his coach. There, Graves had used his analytical skills of psychology. In order to be able to achieve a more precise analysis, Graves brought an 8-mm camera to film the drives.

Jeffrey Greene, who graduated from Union College in 1965, shares another anecdote. He has clear memories of Graves' psychology lectures. These were always scheduled early in the morning and it was the charming personality of Graves that had motivated him to rise at such an early hour in order to make it to the lecture on time.

In reference to his theory, Graves mainly classified himself at the red (3, C-P) and blue (4, D-Q) levels.

Graves repeatedly emphasized that achieving the highest possible level in his model did not matter. Instead, individual adaptation to one's environment and circumstances was the deciding factor in leading a successful life.

TABULAR OVERVIEW

EDUCATIONAL BACKGROUND

- B.A. Union College, Mathematics and Sciences, 1940
- M.A. Western Reserve University, Psychology, 1943
- Ph.D. Western Reserve University, Psychology, 1945

WORK EXPERIENCE

1940–42 Teaching assistant, Western Reserve University, Cleveland, Ohio

1942–43 Technical assistant, Personnel Research Institute of Western Reserve University

1943–45 Criminal Psychologist, Cuyahoga County, Ohio

1943–45 Instructor, Psychology, Fenn College

1943–45 Instructor, Psychology, Case Institute of Technology

1945–46 Assistant Professor, Case Institute of Technology

1943–46 Clinical Psychologists, Cleveland Rehabilitation Centre

1945–46 Assistant Professor, Psychology, Western Reserve University, Cleveland, Ohio

1948–56 Associate Professor, Psychology, Union College Schenectady, New York

1956–78 Professor, Union College

ADVISORY ACTIVITIES

1943–48 Consultation of various business organizations and companies including Dresser Industries, Apex Vacuum, ALCOA, and GM, He was also a clinical advisor at the Cuyahoga County and Ohio State prisons.

1948 Clinical Advisor of the Juvenile Court of the State of New York. Advisor for clinical childhood, adolescent, and geriatric issues at Ellis Hospital, Schenectady, New York.

1950–62 Clinical Physiological Advisor, Schenectady Rehabilitation Centre.

1957–63 Advisor, New York Bell System and personnel practices and problems. Consultation of various business organizations and companies including the USDA, the Department of Welfare and Institutions, the State of Virginia, the New York State Department of Civil Service, and the New York State Department of Mental Hygiene.

THE DEVELOPMENT OF HIS THEORY

This part of the book is based on Graves' original descriptions of his research, found in the book *Levels of Human Existence* (Graves, 2002). We selected what we consider most important to understand his research journey and partly summarized, partly rephrased his original work.

MOTIVATION AND BEGINNINGS: "SO WHO IS RIGHT?"

Annoyed by the conflicts within psychology, Graves was on the verge of giving up teaching. He no longer had any desire to explain which theories were correct and which were not. This was a central question that students would always ask. However, instead of giving up teaching, Graves became motivated to make the confusion and contradictions of psychological research the basis of his work.

FUNDAMENTAL QUESTIONS: WHAT EXACTLY CONSTITUTES A PSYCHOLOGICALLY SOUND INDIVIDUAL?

What exactly constitutes a psychologically sound individual? With this fundamental question, Graves set about his research. First of all, he formulated some key background questions.

1. Is it possible to demonstrate that conflict, confusion and controversy are represented among the conceptions of psychological health?
2. If this is the case, which conceptions of psychological health exist in the psyche of biologically mature individuals? (the subjects were between 18 and 61 and included both men and women)

3. Do the existing conceptions suggest that psychological health is viewed as an instantaneous mental state, a condition, or a psychological process?
4. What is the nature of psychological health depending on whether it is viewed as an instantaneous mental state or as a condition?
5. If psychological health is viewed as an instantaneous mental state or condition, can confusion and controversies become theoretically understandable and resolvable by creating clarity as to what constitutes the state of psychological health?
6. If psychological health is viewed as a process, can we theoretically develop an understanding for this process which can clarify the troubling confusion and contradiction and suggest theoretical means for resolving this into psychological information, theory and the world of human affairs?

Graves then formulated these fundamental questions as specific research questions for the first phase of his studies:

1. How can we think of biologically mature individuals with respect to healthy personalities?
2. Do biologically mature individuals have a main conception of what constitutes a healthy personality?
3. Do biologically mature individuals have more than one conception of this?
4. If adults have various conceptions of a healthy personality, can these be summarized in groups of similar conceptions?
5. How can the numerous conceptions be classified, if at all?
   a. Can they be classified based on content? – If so, how?
   b. Can they be structurally classified? – If so, how?
   c. Can they be functionally classified? – If so, how?

Do individuals with similar conceptions react in a similar or different manner in similar or different situations?

6. Will there be evidence that one conception of the healthy personality proves to be superior to another conception?

In summary, Graves formulated the fundamental questions as follows:

"What will be the nature and the character of conceptions of psychological health of biologically mature human beings who are intelligent but relatively unsophisticated in psychological knowledge in general, and theory of personality, in particular?"

(Graves, 2002, p 11)

DATA COLLECTION

Because Graves was fully occupied with teaching at the university, he saw his students as the only possibility of collecting data for his research. Therefore, within the first five weeks of his course on "normal personality", he instructed them not to read anything about this topic and to rather discuss it as part of the course and to exchange ideas. Then, at the end of these five weeks, they were to write a one-page essay on their personal conception of a psychologically healthy human personality. He repeated this method in eight separate groups. Within the second five weeks, he divided his class into random groups in which the students presented their own conceptions and questioned and commented on those of others. Graves sat behind a one-way mirror so that he could observe the behavior of the presenters while they were critiqued and questioned by the other students. At the end of these five weeks, the students were to defend or modify their original concepts based on their experiences in the groups. Graves was thereby able to determine whether their concepts had changed under the influence of their fellow students. In the third round, the students learned something about various authorities and their concepts on the topic of healthy personality. At the end of this third round, they were again asked to defend or modify their own conception.

QUESTIONS FOR FURTHER STUDY

Based on his first data collection, Graves posted the following questions for further study:

1. What happens to the conception of healthy human behavior if the individual is criticized by another individual who has his or her own conception of healthy human behavior?
2. Moreover, what will happen when a person with a conception of healthy human behavior is given the task of comparing this with a conception developed by an authority in the field?
3. How will students behave if their fellow students criticize them?

At that time, the basic data consisted of three sets:

1. The basic data in the form of the original conceptions.
2. The modifications and defence under the pressure of the fellow students.
3. The modifications and defence when being influenced by authority.

The data collected by Graves showed some interesting results

1. An impressive study of particular personal beliefs about the nature of healthy human behavior.
2. Reactions to the criticism of fellow classmates, which was expressed in the modification or defence of the original conceptions.
3. The interaction and responsiveness of the individuals as they are criticized by fellow students, which was secretly observed and documented from behind a one-way mirror and an intercommunication system.
4. The relation to confrontation with authority as shown by the defended or modified conceptions.
5. Some interview data from discussions on randomly chosen topics after the students had prepared their original conceptions and the two reworked versions. Graves sat down with them to discuss why they had made the changes.

DATA PROCESSING

Graves took the original conceptions, gave them to an external group and asked them to classify them in some manner. That was the only instruction. Each year, a new group was assigned with this task and the collection of data became more extensive from year to year. It was therefore a cumulative process.

In the first year, the jurors arrived at two main classifications of healthy personalities – two categories with two sub-types each. Over 60% of the original material could be classified into categories with the following principles: (1) self-rejection/self-sacrifice is healthy or (2) self-expression is healthy.

These categories were confirmed year after year even though the new jurors were not aware of the classifications of the previous jurors.

At this point in his research, Grave noticed that he had come across something meaningful even though he was unaware of where this would lead him.

The two categories with two sub-types each can be described as follows:

I. Deny/sacrifice self category
   i. Deny/sacrifice self now to get reward later (later blue, 4, D-Q)
   ii. Deny/sacrifice self to get acceptance now (later green, 6, F-S)

II. Express self category
   i. Express self as self desires in a calculating fashion and at the expense of others (later orange, 5, E-R)
   ii. Express self as self desires but not at the expense of others (later yellow, 7, A'-N')

With these four sub-types, Graves began to determine a relationship between the three studies about criticism from fellow students, classifications by authority and interactions with fellow students.

He determined that students of the sub-type *deny/sacrifice self now for later reward* defended their position in the second version of their essay after receiving critique from fellow students. In the next round, however, the students changed their essays under the influence of an authority. This differed from students in the *deny/sacrifice self now in order to receive acceptance now* category. For them, it was the other way around.

A very important aspect of the model, the switch between the I- and we-reference, was clearly established from the data. *Deny/sacrifice now* always changed to *express self* and *express self* always changed to *deny/sacrifice self now* if the change took place centrally. Graves comes to an important distinction: that between *central* and *peripheral* (subordinate, *author's note*) change. The latter always takes place in one system or one category. On the other hand, central change means a switch to one of the other three systems or categories.

The students in the *express self in a calculated manner and at the expense of others* category were influenced neither by their fellow students nor by the authorities. They also expressed little interest in other positions. They had a great need for freedom, felt constrained and wanted the others to specify a position. In the small groups, they often tried to assume leadership and to use what they had learned to their advantage. In contrast, the *express self without doing this at the expense of others* group allowed themselves to be influenced by both their fellow students and the authorities and reconsidered their concepts. This group also never complained about the method used or other established rules.

In time, there was a clear pattern in the change of the conceptions: *Deny/sacrifice now to get reward later* (later blue, 4, D-Q) switched to *express self as self desires in a calculating fashion and at the expense of others* (later orange, 5, E-R), switched to *deny/sacrifice to get acceptance now* (later green, 6 F-S), switched to *express self as self desires without doing this at the expense of others* (later yellow, 7, A'-N ')

In 1959, Graves was met with a great surprise because the previous highest category, *self-expression without doing this at the expense of others* (later yellow, 7, A'-N'), appeared to change. This corresponded to both the highest level of Maslow's hierarchy of needs, the self-actualizing individual, as well as the fully functioning personality according to Rogers, the declared goal of human development. Some people began to question this idea of a healthy human personality, which resulted in an additional, previously unavailable conception: *Deny/sacrifice self for existential reality.* The conditions that were presented as an ultimatum in the theories of Maslow and Rogers were thus uncertain. This generally questioned psychological health as a condition and suggested that it was rather an open process. Another conception, *impulsive self-expression at any price* (later red, 3, C-P), also derived from the data and was added.

The data of the least years was re-examined. It turned out that the new category switched to *deny/sacrifice now for later reward* (later blue, 4, D-Q). *Deny/sacrifice self for existential reality* (later turquoise, 8, B'-O') followed the category *express self as self desires but not at the expense of others* (later yellow, 7, A'-N').

Psychological health therefore seemed to be an open, hierarchical process. At this point, Graves realized that he was not only concerned with psychological health but also with small personality systems. On this basis, he continued his research.

CONTINUING RESEARCH

To obtain further explanations for his hypothetical personality systems, Graves divided his students into groups according to the similarity of their original conceptions and conducted a series of psychological tests, thereby observing their organization and ways of working.

In doing so, he yielded the following data:

1. The group results of standardized tests.

2. How the groups organized themselves during problem solving (Graves left this up to the groups).
3. How individuals with similar concepts interact with each other.
4. How individuals with similar concepts work towards resolving problems.
5. The average time groups needed to find answers.
6. How many solutions the groups found.
7. The quality of the answers.
8. Average time required to find solutions (for specified types of questions).

For the measured properties, Graves then created rankings of the respective mean values based on the four original concepts, e.g. for *cognitive complexity* and *intelligence*. It was found that cognitive complexity increased from each level to the next, i.e. each additional level was more complex than the previous one. However, intelligence was evenly distributed across all levels. Some characteristics were dominant in only one level. Others increased from level to level or vice versa. Some developed in a cyclical manner, which became a central aspect of the model. In other words, the value of a property was high on one level and low on the following level and then high again on the following level and so on.

LET THE DATA TALK

The following diagrams show these moderate types across the four levels in relation to the characteristics and abilities that Graves had measured in his investigations. The line thus shows the respective development that occurs during the switch from one existential level to the next. (Data Source: Graves (2002) p. 127-130)

AUTONOMY

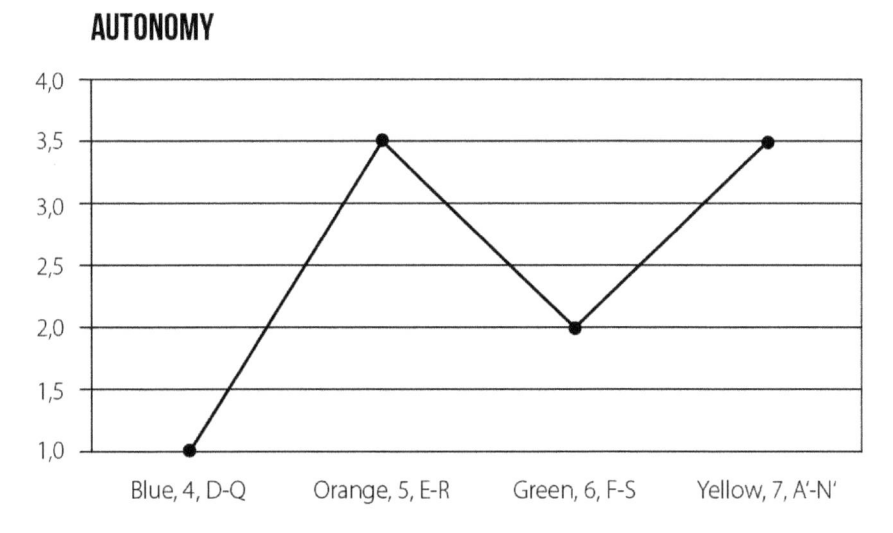

Figure 7: Autonomy

Autonomy is especially pronounced in the I-related orange (5, E-R) and yellow (7, A'-N') levels, i.e. categories in which the self is expressed. The lowest values can be found for blue (4, D-Q). At this level, loyalty plays a large role, the connection with private systems and enterprises. Individuals at the green level (6, F-S) are team-oriented and somewhat more autonomous; several opinions are possible here.

INTELLIGENCE

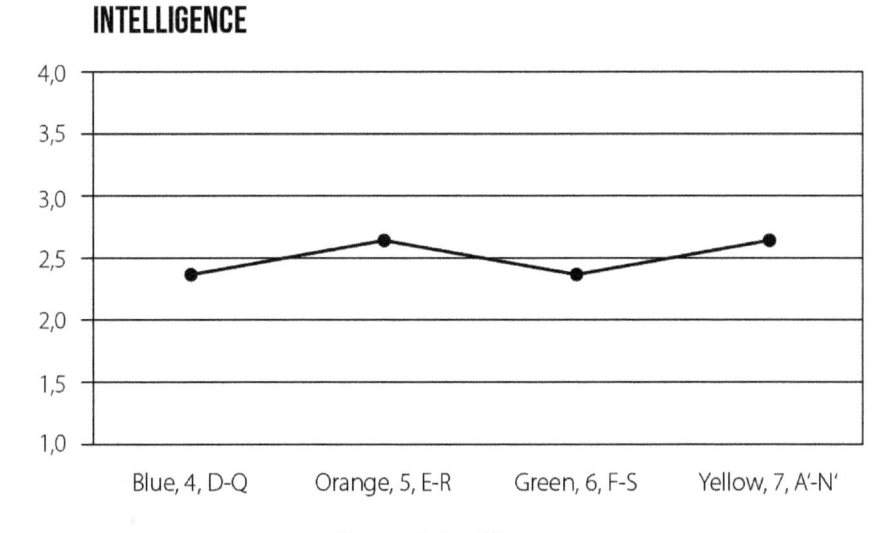

Figure 8: Intelligence

Intelligence is evenly divided over all levels. Value systems do not play a role.

AUTHORITATIVE ATTITUDE

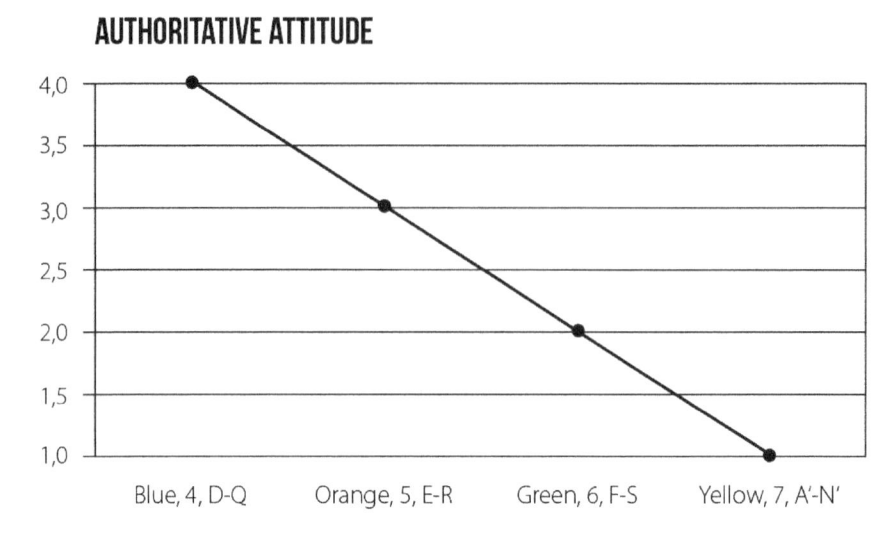

Figure 9: Authoritative attitude

The authoritative attitude, i.e. the willingness to sub-ordinate authorities to hierarchically higher rules and regulations, steadily decreases across the levels.

ACHIEVING NEW CONCEPTS

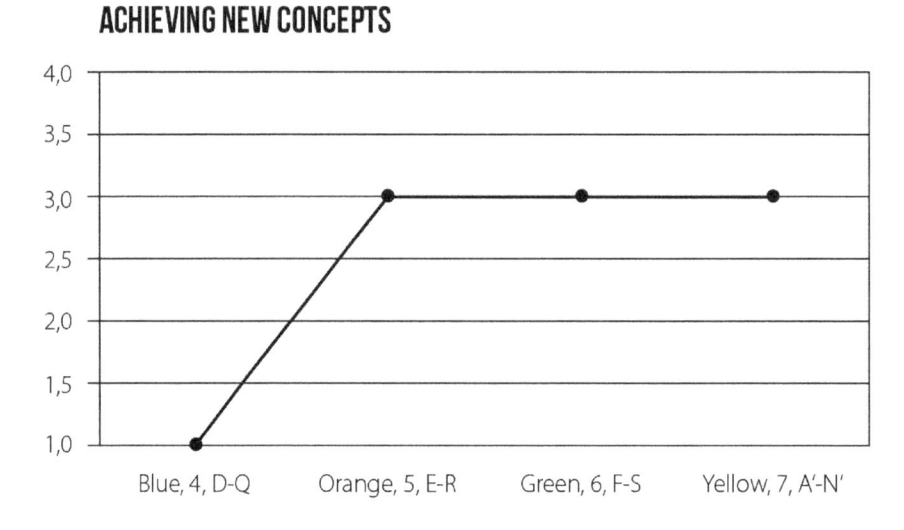

Figure 10: Achieving new concepts

This involves reassembling things in order to arrive at a new concept. Blue (4, D-Q) has a very low value, while the other three levels equally facilitate arriving at new concepts.

CREATING INNOVATIONS

Figure 11: Creating innovations

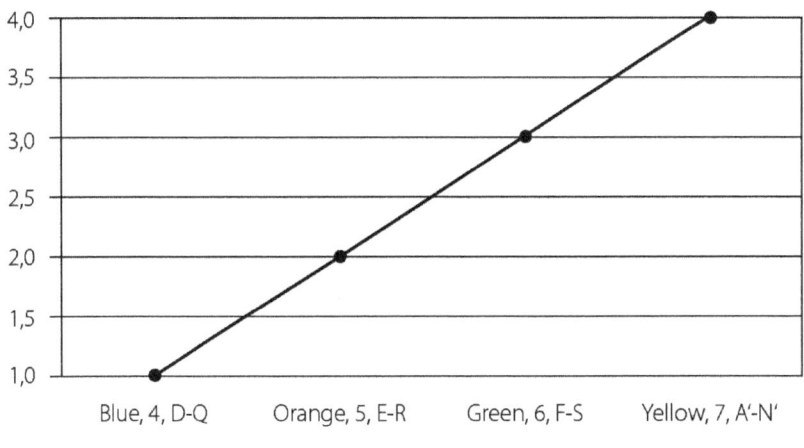

Creating innovation required creative new behavior. Here, the values increased in a linear manner, with yellow (7, A'-N') being the most successful.

SELF-CONTROL

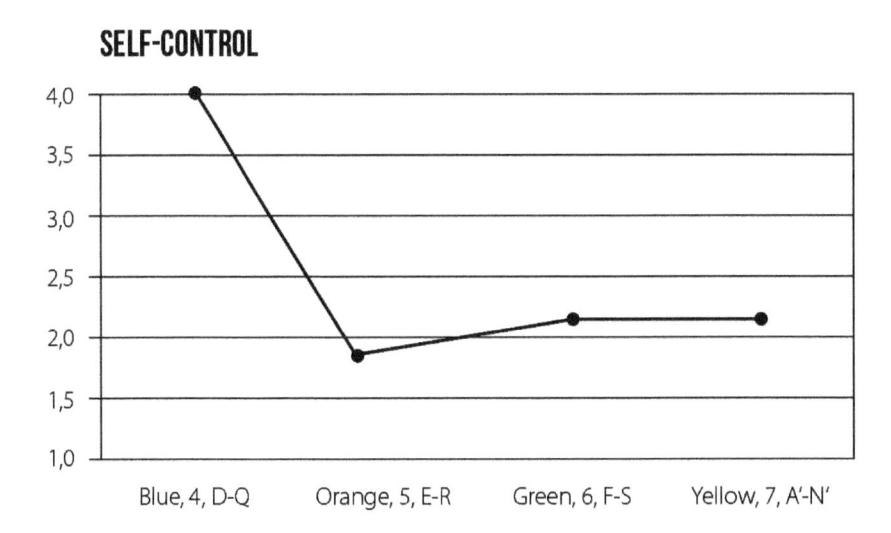

Figure 12: Self-control

While the blue level (4, D-Q) had the lowest values for autonomy, it clearly has the highest average for self-control, which is an entirely contrasting construct. For the other three levels, it is approximately equally distributed.

BELONGING

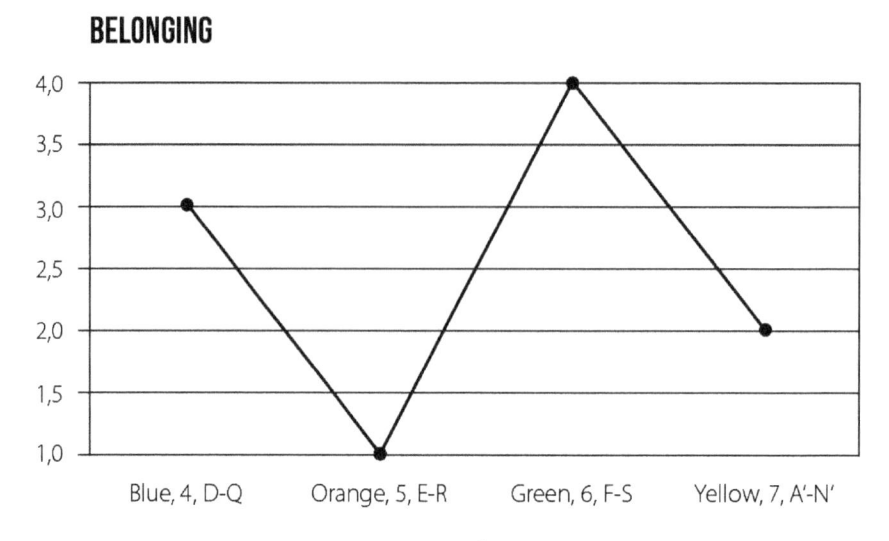

Figure 13: Belonging

At the blue level (4, D-Q), belonging is an important value. However, there are clearly defined boundaries here. It is larger at the green level (6, F-S), as it is also connected with an emotional conviction. It is the least pronounced at the orange level (5, E-R), where personal goals and success are at the forefront. Where and with whom these are achieved is secondary. The yellow level (7, A'-N') is more flexible here. At times, people on this level get involved in an authentic way. At other times, they are more than happy by themselves.

AGGRESSION

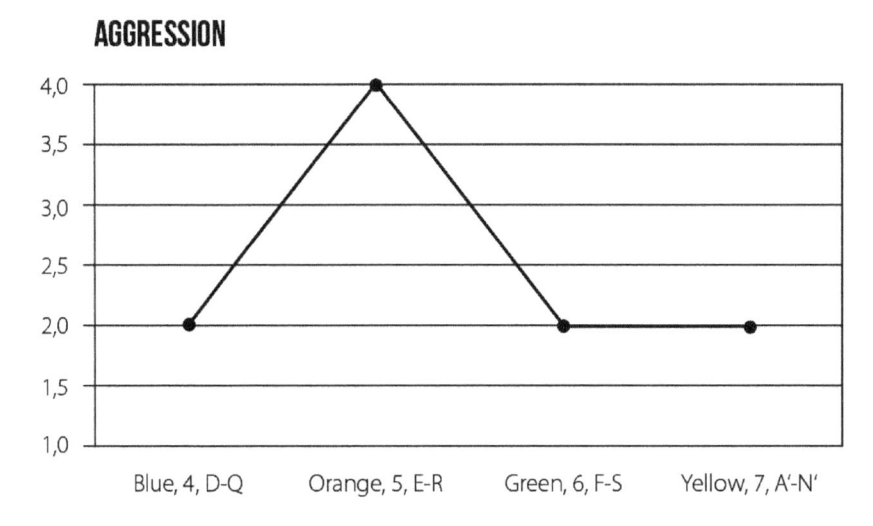

Figure 14: Aggression

At the blue (4, D-Q), green (6, F-S) and yellow (7, A'-N') levels, aggression is roughly equally pronounced and is in the middle range. Here, the orange level (5, E-R) is the outlier. This does not, however, involve physical aggression but rather the extent to which opposing points of view are attacked, the extent to which one's opinion is expressed over another and the extent of public criticism and contradiction as well as how quickly one gets angry.

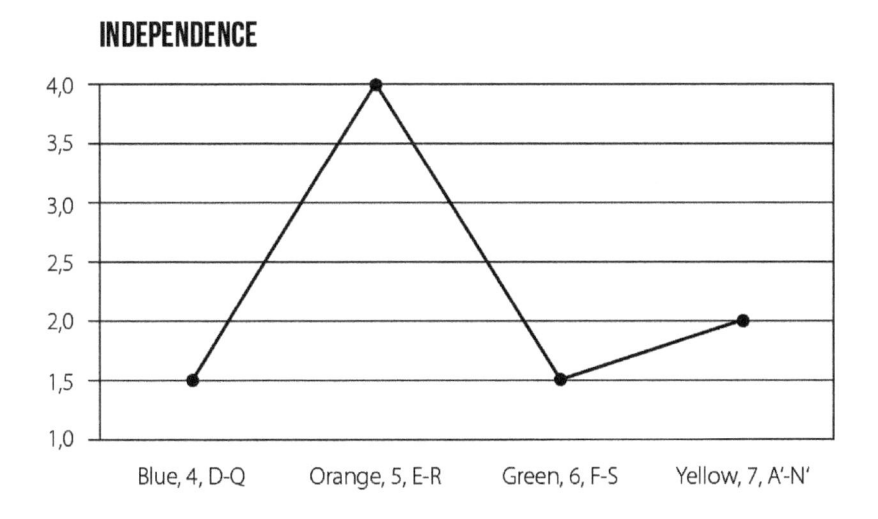

INDEPENDENCE

Figure 15: Independence

Independence pertains to how much individuals trust themselves to express their own opinions, make independent decisions, criticize authorities and do unconventional things as well as the extent to which responsibilities and obligations are perceived. The highest values are clearly seen for the orange level (5, E-R). Yellow (7, A'-N') followed far behind because a relativistic, less absolute expression prevails at this level. Blue (4, D-Q) and green (6, F-S) are alike and have the lowest values, albeit for different reasons. Like orange, blue is quite absolute. Green is open to differing opinions and values them but is less independent because of the desire for harmony and consensus.

CONCEPTUALIZATION

The conceptualization was derived directly from Graves' processed data, which stated the following:

a) Conceptualized adult behavior is such that there is no variation between psychological dimensions such as intelligence or temperament.
b) Conceptualized adult behavior is such that quantitative variation in some dimensions is possible: authority and dogmatism.
c) Conceptualized adult behavior takes the form of a reciprocal wave as well as a custom that allows the repetition of motives: the change data and organizational data.
d) Conceptualized adult behavior is such that each additional system is similar yet simultaneously different to its alternative: the change data.
e) Conceptualized adult behavior is such that each system has its own specification and its own quality: the interaction data.
f) Conceptualized adult behavior is such that certain systems tend to be externally oriented while others tend to be internally oriented.
g) Conceptualized adult behavior is such that the degree of behavior-related freedom increases with every system.

CYCLICAL

The cyclical dimension of the model is an important factor that had not played a role in the previous and rather static personality models. There was regular switching between self-sacrifice and self-expression. For Graves, this was associated with the fact that some individuals attempt to adjust themselves to their environments, while others attempt to adjust the environment to their ideas. Here, there is also an alternation between adaptation/growth and plateau/consolidation. Today, this is designated as I-relation and we-relation.

This alternation can be clearly seen in the double helix graphic of Graves. The x-axis depicts the existential problems that individuals face regarding their personal psychological time. The y-axis depicts the various existential states or levels in which individuals can be found. There are two waved lines. The first line represents the existential level at which systems adjust to their environment and do not attempt to change it. The second line represents all existential levels at which the systems adjust the environment to meet their own ideas.

A further aspect of the theory is that freedom increases from level to level in the form of numbers of choices. This is why the systems also increase in size as they move upward. Because of the enormous change and high increase in complexity, the yellow level (7, G-T or A'-N') had to be depicted as large as +all previous levels combined.

NEUROLOGICAL SYSTEMS

Graves assumed that the brain creates neurological systems in a hierarchical and dynamic manner and that it was designed to solve the particular set of problems of the current level.

These were one aspect of the development. On the other hand were the living conditions, the environment, or the existential problems, which also exhibited a cyclical change.

Together, the neurological systems and living conditions constituted the existential conditions.

The learning process is different at each level:

- Beige (1, A-N): Habit
- Purple (2, B-O): Pavlovian/classical conditioning
- Red (3, C-P): Operant/instrumental conditioning
- Blue (4, D-Q): Avoidance conditioning
- Orange (5, E-R): Expectancy learning
- Green (6, F-S): Operational learning process

Thus, different systems react to different stimuli. Certain types of learning only function at certain levels and no longer function at others.

MOVEMENT THROUGH THE SYSTEMS/LEVELS

For this, Graves used the image of a Christmas tree with a string of lights for which the brightness of individual lights can be regulated. Thus, if an individual is at the beige level, the lowest level of lights is quite bright, while the lights above it are dimmed. There is no switching on or off but rather the dimming of lights or levels, i.e. the intensity of the level shifts; it increases for one and simultaneously decreases for other levels.

PSYCHOPATHOLOGY

Graves also questioned which forms of psychopathology were created at which levels, which symptoms were typical and which treatments were appropriate for them.

The manner of dealing with environmental challenges continues to develop and becomes more complex. For example, it can manifest itself in certain forms of psychological pathology and types of crime.

In any case, the therapist should be at a higher level than the patient is but not too widely removed because he or she may react ineffectively. As examples, Graves cites famous therapists such as Freud, Jung and Adler, who all had preferences regarding their patients.

ADDITIONAL RESEARCH METHODS

TACHISTOSCOPE

With the help of a so-called tachistoscope, Graves investigated whether individuals recognized certain terms that corresponded to their own value systems more quickly than other terms and also if they recognized them quicker than people with different value systems. A tachistoscope is a device for the standardized measurement of perceptual situations. With this device, it is possible to systematically vary the perceptual material as well as the time the material is presented. A tachistoscope is a device used in perceptual psychology, which is utilized for so-called tachistoscopy. The tachistoscope is constructed in such a way that allows visual stimuli e.g. images or symbols to be briefly presented. The stimuli can be presented for less than a millisecond so that they are only subconsciously perceived.

It was thereby revealed that individuals most quickly detected terms or values that were assigned to their value systems or their levels. Almost in a bell curve like distribution, the detection times increased in both directions, i.e. the further away a level is from one's own main characteristic, the longer it takes until the term is detected. This demonstrated that one's own value systems make a difference in the subconscious processing of information.

A 2012 study by Caspers S, Heim S, Lucas MG, Stephan E, Fischer L, et al. confirmed Graves' results with respect to the differing reaction times.

GRAVES AND MASLOW

Graves and Maslow were contemporaries who were both concerned with adult development. Their models are both hierarchical and divided into various developmental stages. Both viewed the presence of tension as an important factor for growth. Graves attempted to match his data with Maslow's developmental stages, but he was only partially successful.

For Maslow, the highest developmental stage was self-actualization. At the same time, this was also the endpoint or the stated objective. Here the human potential would come to full fruition and a kind of flow feeling would arise. Maslow's concept was thus a closed one.

However, according to Graves' theory, there was a form of self-actualization at every existential level. They were thus unable to present an ideal final state but rather one of many functional forms of being. Graves' system was also open. Instead of an ideal fixed end condition, he was convinced that in the course of human development, additional existential states would always arise, each with their own variations of self-actualization.

For Graves, external factors played at least as great a role in change and growth as internal ones did, whereby there is always a switch from *self-expression* and *self-sacrifice* across the levels. Growth occurred in both cases. Maturity can thus exist in both dependent and independent forms.

In contrast, Maslow believed that growth came more from the inside than the outside, which entailed increasing independence from the environment. For him, a stronger external orientation meant a lower maturity during development towards a psychologically free, independent individual.

This was also reflected in the respective representations: for Maslow, it was a closed hierarchy. For Graves, it was an upwardly open double helix; one helix representing the neurological systems and the other one standing for the changing environment.

Graves wrote that he and Maslow had quarreled for eight years. However, Maslow ultimately recognized both the idea of cyclic development and the existence of multiple systems of expression and belonging. Also, that the system of human development is open, thus allowing for the continuous development of new levels.

CHRONOLOGICAL REPRESENTATION OF HIS WORK AND LECTURES

Chronology of the publications and articles of Clare W. Graves assembled by William R. Lee (http://www.clarewgraves.com/source_content/chron.html):

1945

- "A Study of the Genesis and Dynamics of Psychopathic Personality as Revealed By Combining The Clinical Case History and Experimental Approaches," Doctoral thesis, Case Western University. Listed under Hall, Calvin Springer, Jr., U of Cal. Berkeley, Volume S0028, Number AAI0140317

1959

- "An Emergent Theory of Ethical Behavior Based Upon – An Epigenetic Model," Schenectady, New York, 1959

1960

- "Salient Points for Understanding Human Behavior per the Existential Psychological Point of View," early 1960s – several tables and lists which reflect Dr Graves' thinking at the time

1961

- "On the Theory of Ethical Behavior," presented at the First Unitarian Society of Schenectady, New York, 1961

1962

- "The Implications to Management of Systems – Ethical Theory," 11 November 1962

1964–1965

- "Levels of Human Existence and Their Relation to Value Analysis and Engineering," proceedings of the Fifth Annual Values Analysis Conference, source of presentation unknown – (about 1964–1965)
- "Value Systems and their Relation to Managerial Controls and Organizational Viability," paper presented before the College of Management Philosophy, The Institute of Management Sciences, Jack Tar Hotel, San Francisco, 3 February 1965
- "Personality Structure and Perceptual Readiness" (with B. Huntley and D.W. LaBier) "An Investigation of Their Relationship to Hypothesized Levels of Human Existence," (research carried out by Doug LaBier) at Union College, Schenectady, New York in May 1965.
- "Man: An Enlarged Conception of His Nature," paper presented before the Second Annual Conference on the Cybercultural Revolution at the Hotel Americana in New York City, New York on 27 May 1965.

1966

- Favorite case studies: "Blair Bischel" and "Glenn Spicer" Both of these papers are listed as follows: Cases of John B. Miner, The Management of Ineffective Performance, McGraw-Hill
- "Deterioration of Work Standards," Harvard Business Review – September/October – 1966, Vol.44, No. 5, pages 117–126 (Not available for online reading – reprints from HBR.)
- "On the Theory of Value," presented at the National Institutes of Mental Health, Washington, D.C., March 1967.

1969

- "Motivation Wise, Executives Are Reluctant Dragons," keynote address for the Institute on Motivation and Productivity of the Public Personnel Association, The Hudson-Mohawk Training Directors Society, The Industrial Training Council and The

Capital District Personnel Association, In-Town Motel, Albany, New York, 25 March 1969.
- "A Systems View of Value Problems," IEEE Systems Science & Cybernetics Conference, Philadelphia, PA, October 1969. (revised in later work)

1970

- "Levels of Existence: An Open System Theory of Values," The Journal of Humanistic Psychology, Fall 1970, Vol. 10. No. 2, pp. 131–154. (The publisher does not authorize electronic reproduction. However, a paper reprint is included in the book, "Clare W. Graves: Levels of Human Existence."
- "The Levels of Existence and their Relation to Welfare Problems," paper presented at the Annual Conference Meeting, Virginia State Department of Welfare and Distribution, Roanoke, Virginia, 6 May 1970. (30 pages)
- "Personal Dimensions of Student Disaffection," paper read at the 175th anniversary celebration of the founding of Union College on 7 May 1970
- "The Congruent Management Strategy," with Helen T. Madden & Lynn P. Madden based on an industrial study

1971

- Untitled Presentation by Dr Clare W. Graves, Annual Meeting of The Association of Humanistic Psychology, 1971
- "Levels of Existence Related To Learning Systems," paper read at the Ninth Annual Conference of the National Society for Programming Instruction, Rochester, New York, 31 March 1971
- "Seminar on Levels of Human Existence" at the Washington School of Psychiatry, Washington, D.C., 16 October 1971 (Based on a tape transcription by William Lee, revised February 2002. An expanded and updated paperback version with illustrations and

tables is available from ECLET Publishing as Clare W. Graves: Levels of Human Existence.)
- "How Should Whom Lead Who to Do What?" paper delivered for the YMCA Management Forum of 1971–1972, Downtown Branch YMCA, St. Louis, Missouri, 9 November 1971

1973
- "Let Us Bring Humanistic and General Psychology Together: A Research Project Needing to Become," paper presented at National Institutes of Mental Health in Washington, DC on 16 March 1973
- Seminar Notes, Quetico Centre, Canada, October, 1973

1974
- "Human Nature Prepares for a Momentous Leap," The Futurist magazine, April 1974, pp. 72–87
- Seminar at Quetico Centre, Canada, June, 1974 (audio tapes)
- Seminar at Quetico Centre, Canada, August, 1974 (audio tapes)
- Interview with Cliff McIntosh, Quetico Centre (video tape)

1977
- "What is Life All About? What is it Meant to Be?" (Tentative title for previously unpublished book manuscript to be released 2005 as The Never Ending Quest by ECLET Publishing.)

1978
- "Up the Existential Staircase," seminar on the Development, Nature, Meaning and Management of The Levels of Existence, Emergent, Cyclical, Double Helix Model of Adult Human Psychosocial Coping Systems [1978 / same paper with graphs added 1980]

1980
- Seminar with National Values Centre in Dallas, December, 1980 (audio tape)

1981

- "Summary Statement: The Emergent, Cyclical, Double-Helix Model Of The Adult Human Biopsychosocial Systems," handout for presentation to World Future Society, Boston, Mass., 20 May 1981 (temporary .pdf version)

1982

- Seminar Notes, Quetico Centre, Canada, October, 1973

1986

- Dr Graves' Union College Biography and Obituary as it appeared in the Concordy, 16 January 1986

SUMMARY OF THE ARTICLES

Because of his involvement in various professional fields and his extensive research, Graves was active in many contexts. Accordingly, his articles deal with management styles, learning systems, social assistance, social development and a lot more. Graves' writings are summarized on the following pages. His research and development can be traced in chronological order, thus providing insight into the various application areas of his theory. For the most part, we have avoided redundancies. At certain points however, repetitions make sense because there were numerous small modifications in the description of the individual levels. For example, Graves spoke of eight and sometimes nine developmental stages, whereby at one point, there was a shift of one level. For an easier understanding of the different level designations, all variants are listed, although the focus will be on the colors[4]. Additional designations in the form of digits (1–9) and letter pairs (e.g. A-N and B-O), Graves' original notation, are listed in parentheses.

The following table provides an overview:

Rank/tier	Graves' category	Color	Designation	Orientation, relatedness
Second position Second tier		Coral	none to date	I-related
	B'-O'	Turquoise	Global view	We-related
	A'-N'	Yellow	Flex flow	I-related

---

[4] The Colors were introduced by Chris Cowan in the 1970s and became a common language

First position First tier	F-S	Green	Human bond	We-related
	E-R	Orange	Strive drive	I-related
	D-Q	Blue	Truth force	We-related
	C-P	Red	Power gods	I-related
	B-O	Purple	Kin spirits	We-related
	A-N	Beige	Survival sense	I-related

We begin with two studies that initially had nothing to do with Graves' later theory. The first is his Master's thesis, which concerned the irritability of rats, whilst the second is his doctoral thesis in which he describes a realistic view of the psychopathic personality from different sources. In both works, his extremely critical and exact procedure is highly evident as are his efforts to interconnect different theories and approaches. Even then, he had always insisted on the individual assessment of cases; he avoided universal explanations. This attitude is especially noticeable in his doctoral thesis.

MASTER'S THESIS: INDIVIDUAL DIFFERENCES IN IRRITABILITY IN THE MALE RAT (1943)

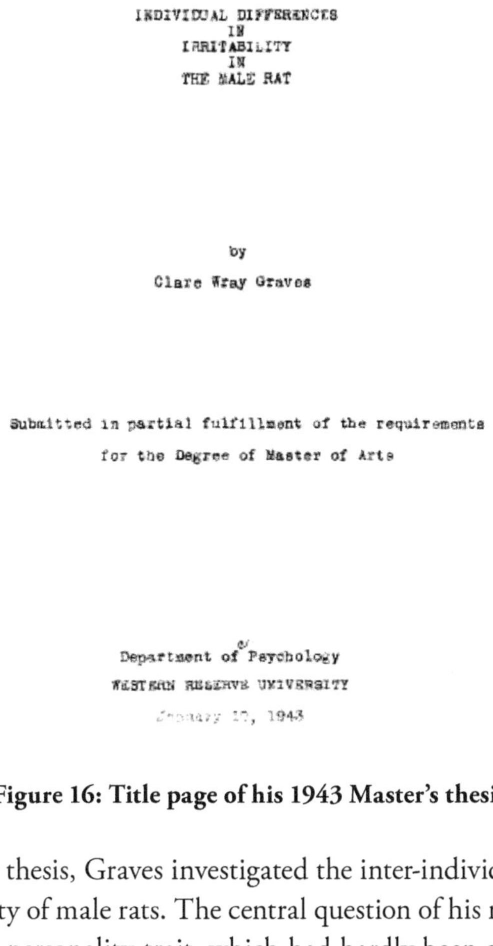

```
INDIVIDUAL DIFFERENCES
         IN
    IRRITABILITY
         IN
    THE MALE RAT




           by
    Clare Wray Graves



Submitted in partial fulfillment of the requirements
      for the Degree of Master of Arts




         Department of Psychology
        WESTERN RESERVE UNIVERSITY
             January 15, 1943
```

Figure 16: Title page of his 1943 Master's thesis

In his Master's thesis, Graves investigated the inter-individual differences in the irritability of male rats. The central question of his research was his interest in this personality trait, which had hardly been studied. Gilbert Van Tassel Hamilton (US physician and author, *author's note*) took the view that animal investigations would lead to conclusions about human personality and associated behavior.

The definition of irritability had to meet two criteria, namely that it (1) described a behavior corresponding to the psychological behavior, which is triggered by a provoking stimulus and (2) applied to the behavior that was investigated in the experiment.

Differences in irritability in relation to the type of rearing, living conditions and age were investigated in 34 rats. He intentionally used rats that were either bred to be timid or fearless as well as ones that were mixed, and albino and hooded rats that were not especially bred. As an irritation or stimulus, a piece of electrical tape was attached to a hind leg and a slight pressure applied. In a period of five minutes, in addition to the qualitative observation of behavior, the following five quantitative factors were measured:

1. The number of attempts to remove the tape.
2. Total time of the attempts.
3. Time passed until the first attempt.
4. Duration of the first attempt.
5. Duration of the last attempt.

Of these five factors, only the number of attempts and the total time (1 and 2) turned out to be satisfactory values for distinction.

Graves was able to find significant differences between the various types of rats. Compared with the fearless rats, the timid rats attempted to remove the tape significantly less frequently, less aggressively and for a shorter time. They were also less aggressive towards the human investigators, while the fearless rats often attempted to bite the investigator and fight them with all their strength as the tape was being attached. The hybrid rats demonstrated an intermediary irritability. Albino rats were less irritable than the hooded rats. Increased age did not reveal any change in the relative characteristics, although the responsiveness of the rats was decreased. An additional "hunger" factor also did not result in any significant change.

There is therefore innate inter-individual variation in irritability. Further investigations were to be performed with relation to fear and anger.

Clare W. Graves

DOCTORAL THESIS: A STUDY OF THE GENESIS AND DYNAMICS OF PSYCHOPATHIC PERSONALITY AS REVEALED BY COMBINING THE CLINICAL CASE HISTORY AND EXPERIMENTAL APPROACHES (1945)

A STUDY OF THE GENESIS AND DYNAMICS
OF PSYCHOPATHIC PERSONALITY AS REVEALED
BY COMBINING THE CLINICAL CASE HISTORY AND
EXPERIMENTAL APPROACHES

by

CLARE WRAY GRAVES

Submitted in partial fulfillment of the requirements
for the Degree of Doctor of Philosophy

Department of Psychology
WESTERN RESERVE UNIVERSITY
August 15, 1945

Figure 17: Title page of the doctoral thesis of Clare W. Graves

In his thesis, Graves devoted himself to a topic of clinical psychology: the psychopathic personality. He started with the provocative statement, that since Philippe Pinel's (French Psychiatrist, *author's note*) "maníaque sans delire" (offender without delusion) paper appeared 136 years ago, the understanding of the psychopathic personality had hardly changed at all. He also noted that different disciplines within psychology cited different reasons for the development of a psychopathic personality. He therefore posed the following primary thesis for his investigation. Assuming that the scientific integrity of the respective theory was upheld, wasn't it possible that they were all correct? Using a combination of experimental, clinical and approaches based on case studies, Graves wanted to determine whether the reasons for these widely divergent conclusions were a matter of the original approach to the problems of the human species. Moreover, if various psychopathic personalities react to one type of therapy but others do not – even though they showed the same behavior – is this based on their different evolutionary histories and the dynamics of their illness?

For this, he conducted a study with three specifically selected groups as well as several subjects that did not belong to any category. All subjects had to cope with tasks under various stress conditions. Group 1 included psychopathic personalities. Group 2 were criminals without nervous or mental disorders and served as the control group. Group 3 were high school students who displayed poor performance and were used to standardize the technique. The technique involved placing the subjects in stressful situations with mild to strong pressure and collecting data from these varying situations. Three levels of expected situations, a persistence task and a task generated from the Wechsler–Bellevue scale for adolescents and adults were adjusted to the stressful situation and used as experimental instruments.

The groups of subjects were assembled by a forensic psychiatrist, a psychiatric social worker and a psychologist (investigator). They were informed that a positive recommendation by the clinic depended solely on their performance in the experimental situation and the satisfaction of the investigator. The variation of the stress levels had been clearly demonstrated in previous studies.

Both individual and group analyses were performed. In the same subjects using the same instruments, varying the level of the expectation situation led to differing results.

There was a fairly clear correlation between the results of one task of an expectation level that required low knowledge and a task that required extensive knowledge. It was thus revealed that psychopathic personalities were less predictable and less persistent than "normal" ones. In addition, they appeared to be disproportionately influenced by success and failure. Instead of also interpreting the stages of the expectation levels as such, they understood the tasks as assessment situations that contained none, little, or a high component of chance.

On the one hand, the interpretation of the results revealed that the analysis of group results did not allow satisfactory conclusions. For the individual subjects, the image that resulted from the evaluation of the tasks, the clinical impression and the case studies was entirely congruent. On the other hand, the divergent perspectives appeared to have resulted from not recognizing that identical behavior can have a variety of origins and be dynamically organized.

It was thus revealed that, compared to the "normal" ones, psychopathic personalities behaved in an irrational manner in stressful situations. Although all psychopathic personalities displayed this irrationality in various degrees, the patterns of the individuals were all different. It was determined that each pattern made sense when considered according to the individual case history and particular clinical presentation.

Graves concluded that the experimental approach was able to show that certain general characteristics exist in the form of observable behavior. He also determined that the same behavior could have diverse origins and is uniquely organized. The psychopathic personality can thus be viewed as a comprehensive general trait with a uniquely organized dynamic.

AN EMERGENT THEORY OF ETHICAL BEHAVIOR – BASED UPON AN EPIGENETIC MODEL (1959)

Starting with criticizing existing theories of ethical behavior, Graves then demonstrates why a new theory was required and established additional criteria that he considered to be indispensable for an adequate theory of ethical behavior.

Graves believed that there was a lack of basic scientific knowledge of ethics as well as of how to resolve ethical problems. Based on their idea of what ethical behavior is, many try to develop something like an ethically sensitive, mature decision-maker.

The *emergent ethical theory* model is based on the concept of epigenetics, (a specialized field of biology that deals with the development of cells and the inheritance of characteristics, *author's note*), the concept of dynamic neurological systems and the trigger.

Graves assumes that ethical behavior can evolve or regress, remain as it is, or change. The basis is essentially established in human neurological systems and is activated by external circumstances. According to Graves, this takes place in various overlapping levels that become increasingly more complex. At the same time, he views life circumstances as a limiting factor that has a large influence on the development of the individual.

For Graves, the first level is amoral. Each one that follows has its own topic with specific values and ideas about what is right or wrong. A change in circumstances slowly results in the development of a new level that reacts to the change.

ON THE THEORY OF ETHICAL BEHAVIOR (1961)

Graves constitutes that the current designation of behavior as moral or amoral is based on the assumptions that (1) there is a rational ethical system, (2) this system builds on good values, and (3) these values are the best principles by which people should live.

Graves challenges these assumptions and finds that historical data does not support the assumption of a rational ethical system and that a new frame of reference permits a more sophisticated approach.

Based on Maslow's hierarchy of needs, he discusses the various stages of development and describes the corresponding value systems. Further development will only take place once the needs of one level have been fulfilled.

Graves distinguished between two different types of values: On one hand, there are values that are good for somebody on a particular needs level, but not if he or she is on a higher level or in the process of reaching it. On the other hand, there are values that belong to every level and which are good for individuals at any given time and place.

Graves connects the needs levels with the ethical development and depicts both as complex, wave-like phenomena. Because of the wave form, elements from various levels are always present. With the creation of each following wave, a part of the preceding wave disappears.

This growth is not a linear process. Instead it reaches a certain point where regression and reorganization occur, before a higher level of ethical behavior is created.

According to his theory, each need level is connected to a system of ethics. Graves describes each step and states typical values for the individual levels. These needs and systems of ethics determine the thoughts and behavior of humans.

Immoral behavior entails demanding someone to behave in a manner in which he or she is not yet ready for; or preventing somebody from reaching the next level, even though he or she is ready to do so; or behavior at higher levels that demonstrates a lack of understanding for lower levels.

There are societies at all levels with mixed levels as well as individuals at different and mixed levels.

Rainer Krumm & Benedikt Parstorfer

THE IMPLICATIONS TO MANAGEMENT OF SYSTEMS-ETHICAL THEORY (1962)

In this article, Graves describes the basis of his theory and then explains its relevance to management.

He considers ethical behavior as a growth phenomenon with definable, overlapping phases that proceed in a certain order – from fewer complexes to more complex phases.

The fulfillment and development of human behavior depends on the respective environment, i.e. life conditions.

In humans, there is a type of innate ethical nature, which is evoked via certain life circumstances in the form of one or another ethical system.

It is an interaction of the intellectual, motivational, emotional, perceptual and ethical systems, all of which are mutually in contact. These are sub-categories of the dynamic cerebral system. If there is a change in only one of these systems, it must be very strong in order to initiate restructuring in all other systems. The view of right and wrong is different in each ethical system.

Graves then describes a total of eight individual ethical systems. This does not correspond to the final order of the levels. The later purple level (2, B-O) is missing in this description. There have also been shifts. The current designations have therefore been listed with corresponding information in parentheses. He does not acknowledge any ethic for the lowest level (beige, 1, A-N) because here, individuals are only concerned with survival. At the second level (later red, 3, C-P), when survival is guaranteed, the rights of the stronger apply. Those who are powerful dictate morality. The third level (later blue, 4, D-Q) can be described by conformist ethics. The group decides what is right and wrong; selfish behavior is considered bad. At the fourth level (later orange, 5, E-R), materialism comes into effect. Having and doing are good, as is being independent. Preventing others from doing or being so, is bad. The fifth level is governed by the prevailing reality, the cognitive ethic, which is based on knowledge (later orange, 5, E-R). The sixth level (later green, 6, F-S) involves the ethics of sympathy in which empathy plays a large role. Graves describes the seventh level (later turquoise, 8, B'-N') as that of aw. It is characterized by deep respect and admiration for the beauty of life. The eighth level (later yellow, 7, A'-N') is the infinite level with a human ethic, which is accompanied by an all-encompassing appreciation for the self and can perceive all other values in order of importance.

Graves then makes the link to management. He first notes that the challenges of managers change with the further development of systems, because individuals think differently and develop other ideas about what is right and wrong, about structures and ways of working. Certain managerial styles only function at the corresponding levels and will be misunderstood at others. Sensitization of managers is therefore important so that they can learn to better assess and manage other individuals and their needs.

LEVELS OF HUMAN EXISTENCE AND THEIR RELATION TO VALUE ANALYSIS AND ENGINEERING (1964–65)

Graves then addresses the problems that he currently sees in the analysis of values and which he designates as the fourth generation of problems, because a type of evolution of challenges takes place. Graves calls the four central points (1) too narrow thinking, (2) the implementation in management, (3) increasing the benefits of value analysis, and (4) the extension of its application to other areas. He views the fifth stage of problems as a redefinition of philosophy and the techniques for enabling the adaptation and expansion of the concepts to new areas.

Graves describes two changes in psychological thinking that influence the area of value analysis. On the one hand, the concept of humans as avoiders of pain and seekers of pleasure is discarded. At this point, the switch between the build-up and release of tension leads to the desired condition. On the other hand, individuals are sometimes so confused about what they think and want, that they try to maintain the status quo and avoid changes or similar. This especially applies to individuals at the lower levels.

"Levels of Human Existence" is the newly evolving concept about how individuals behave. A change in life conditions results in a change in the psychology of the individuals. These changes take place in a certain hierarchical order.

Graves describes the first five levels as subsistence levels because they entail compensating for deficiencies in order to obtain what is required. The additional levels are described as levels of being because they entail growth and motives of expression.

After Graves once again explains the individual levels, he describes the introduction of policies in a company. This introduction was done using fourth-level methods for employees who were also at this level. But how would such a change be incorporated at the various levels? How can the individuals at these levels best be brought closer together? While order and increased pressure bring about change at the fourth level, participatory management is required at the fifth level. The sixth level entails discussing the possibilities for change. If these are found to be plausible, one will get there by oneself.

Graves then asked how the value analysis could be applied in practice and implemented as a managerial tool. The action levels of the organization would first be assessed in order to determine for which problems the concepts of value analysis are applied. Then they would be appropriately implemented at the respective levels.

Clare W. Graves

VALUE SYSTEMS AND THEIR RELATION TO MANAGERIAL CONTROLS AND ORGANIZATIONAL VIABILITY (1965)

In this article, Graves is concerned with why certain ethical values rank above others, the conditions under which this is the case and how these norms influence the survival of organizations.

He starts with some statements from Mason Haire's book, *The Psychology of Management*. According to him, enterprises are also social institutions and part of society. The strategies and actions must therefore reflect the values of society. The questions of how hard one should work and how much commitment can be expected from others are therefore tightly connected with the societal values and the individual self-images. To what extent are there competitive advantages or disadvantages for corporate philosophies that more closely or more poorly match these values? Haire concludes that the freedom of the manager depends on the harmony between social values and those of management. According to Graves, he neglects the fact that there are several ethical systems and that at any time several of these systems can be described and assigned in an organization and in a society.

Graves emphasizes that (1) in most societies, there tends to be several value systems, i.e. something like social values, (2) the congruence and not the similarity of values is the deciding factor for the vitality of an organization, (3) the question of "may" and "may-not" in a working context lies mainly within an organization and not in relation to societal values, (4) the value systems of the manager determine the decisions of the management and the value systems of the employees determine how they react to these decisions, and (5) managers of unhealthy organizations can question the extent to which problems are created as a result of the opposing values of management and employees.

Doing something about the health of companies at the level of values requires a framework in which systematic thinking and the generation of verifiable hypotheses is enabled.

The various existential levels, of which Graves describes nine, determine the nature and character of the value system, the degree of behavioral freedom and the evaluation of behavior as ethical or non-ethical. Higher levels are associated with greater freedom of choice. Even if the human organism tends to psychologically develop in an ordered and hierarchical manner, under certain circumstances, a condition stabilizes at one level or at a combination of several levels.

Graves illuminates the challenges of organizations with the first four existential levels.

The beige level (1, A-N) does not play a role in management, because it is purely concerned with survival. Enterprises and industry do not yet exist at this level.

The purple level (2, B-O) entails creating a secure, predictable and stable world in which everything is determined and roles are defined. God-like authority dictates this order. Both leaders and followers sacrifice themselves. Leaders do this to protect and followers to support the leaders.

A few start moving towards the red level (3, C-P), which makes them feel superior to others. The right of the fittest takes a foothold and with it the ethics of power. At this level, the leadership style is directive management.

However, by increasing their skills and their standard of living, more and more workers are reaching the red level (3, C-P) where management is also situated. This could severely jeopardize the viability of the enterprise. The values are similar, but they are not congruent. Some managers therefore begin to develop towards the blue level (4, D-Q). An existential level characterized by belonging and equality now develops. There is little call for individual thinking, being different, or being guided from within. There are clear rules for right and wrong behavior. Participatory management fits together with the ethics and is now the leading form of control. This form of management provides followers with influence and leaders with acceptance, which is once again congruent. If management and employees are at the blue level (4, D-Q), these processes become so slow that any development stops.

Graves demonstrates that most managers remain at the red (3, C-P) or blue level (4, D-Q), whereby some employees have already developed further. These slow down their employees. The managers at the red level fear for their power and the managers at the blue level fear not being liked.

The theory sees no great value in the development of universal institutional, cultural and social values. There will always be a mixture of different value systems and these should be adapted to.

Which type of creative innovations does a challenged organization require and which individuals at which level are required to implement such innovations? For Graves, this was a deciding question. Conflicts that can be traced back to incongruent values of managers and employees must be resolved.

The solution will be in a form or organization that utilizes the existing differences.

WITH HUNTLEY AND LABIER: PERSONALITY STRUCTURE AND PERCEPTUAL READINESS: AN INVESTIGATION OF THEIR RELATIONSHIP TO HYPOTHESIZED LEVELS OF HUMAN EXISTENCE (1965)

Huntley and LaBier examined the association of personality structure and readiness to perceive based on the detection time of value-related terms. For this, they used a tachistoscope. This is a device for the standardized measurement of perceptual situations. With the tachistoscope, it is possible to systematically vary the perceptual material and the time it is presented. In particular, the pre-attentive perception is examined, i.e. a preconscious, subliminal perception of sensory stimuli. A stimulus is indeed perceived by the nervous system and an effect is triggered. However, this does not penetrate into the consciousness; it is only processed pre-consciously or subconsciously. Other studies have shown that individuals recognized those terms that corresponded to their values much more quickly than those that contradicted their values. So-called taboo words were also recognized significantly more slowly than neutral or positive words. They then transferred these findings to Graves' levels of human existence. They hypothesized that individuals at a given level associated with these value terms, would detect these more quickly than other terms and also more quickly than individuals at a different main level.

Levels three to six were investigated. These correspond to the following current levels: blue (4, D-Q), orange (5, E-R), green (6, F-S) and yellow (7, A'-N'). In order to define the affiliation of the subjects, two different questionnaires were used. One was the *Rokeach Dogmatism Scale*. This questionnaire measures general authoritarianism, general authoritarian attitudes and general intolerance. Rokeach's concept of open and closed belief systems allowed a differentiation between levels 3 and 4 (later 4/D-Q and 5/E-R) from levels 5 and 6 (later 6/F-S and 7/A'-N'). In order to differentiate the other levels from each other, items from the *Dogmatism Scale* are mixed with items from the *Gough-Sanford Rigidity Scale*. The Gough-Sanford Scale measures the resistance to changes in individual beliefs and habits, whereas dogmatism refers to the change of whole belief systems.

The four combination groups and the corresponding levels are listed in the following table:

COMBINATION	EXISTENTIAL LEVEL
high rigidity and high dogmatism	3 (later blue, 4, D-Q)
low rigidity and high dogmatism	4 (later orange, 5, E-R)
high rigidity and low dogmatism	5 (later green, 6, F-S)
low rigidity and low dogmatism	6 (later yellow, 7, A'-N')

After all 52 individuals had filled out the questionnaires; the 12 individuals who could most clearly be assigned to one of the four levels were selected (three for each level).

Five terms that clearly represented each level were selected e.g. "security" and "order" for the third level (later blue, 4, D-Q). Using the tachistoscope, the 20 words were randomly presented in the millisecond range. The presentation time was increased until the term was named correctly.

The results indeed showed a clear correlation between detection time and existential levels. Words that were typical of their own level were detected significantly faster than others were. The further away from one's own level, the longer it took to detect the terms. The detection time for individuals at the third level (later blue, 4, D-Q) was the longest for words typical of the sixth level (later yellow, 7, A'-N'). The detection time was somewhat quicker for individuals at the fifth level (later green, 6, F-S) and so forth.

This confirmed the hypothesis that an individual who can be assigned to an existential level recognizes words that represent this level, more quickly than words that represent other levels and thereby supported Graves' theory of development.

DETERIORATION OF WORK STANDARDS (1966)

In this article, which appeared in Harvard Business Review, Graves describes why work standards deteriorate and what can be done about it. According to Graves, the solution for these problems does not involve changing individuals. It does not have to be theory X or theory Y. Rather, the solution lies in a system of far-reaching changes at the organizational level, which can only be initiated by top-level management.

In his view, there are successive levels of human behavior. The deciding factor is ensuring that the type of management matches the behavioral level of the employees. This means that in most organizations, several methods are required at once, which complicates both the conception and implementation.

Graves describes the deterioration of work standards from four different perspectives: (1) organization, (2) decision maker, (3), behavioral research, and (4) organizational psychology.

From the perspective of the organization, the problem occurs if the employees cannot cope with the qualitative and quantitative requirements of the manufacturing. The organization's challenge is to find ways to achieve the required output. This is the task of the decision maker.

From the perspective of the decision maker, the problem has implications in two of its functions: firstly, the formulation of newer alternatives in the case of large changes to the working environment; and secondly, the selection of the formulated alternative(s) that should be acted upon. These functions prove difficult because of unclear and confusing information about the employees. At the same time, the decision maker recognizes that not only problems that are related to the market, materials and technology can change, but also the individual as a producer himself. The decision makers do not know that a deterioration of work standards usually is a result of certain changes in employees.

According to behavioral research, work standards deteriorate if employees oppose managerial control systems. Employees do this if their needs are not fulfilled by the current system. In order to satisfy the same individuals, the manager must change the system in such a way that it once again fulfils their needs. This is an ongoing development, which is why a frame of references is required to enable the constant reorganization of the managerial control system.

From the perspective of organizational psychology, the problem lies in a complex interaction between leaders, control systems and producers.

Graves presents his theory and relates it to the work context. If individuals are at a particular level, they only have the behavioral freedom that this context requires of them. They can only react in a positive way to managerial principles appropriate for this level and negatively to inappropriate managerial principles, which is reflected in the deterioration of work standards. In this case, we should pay particular attention to incongruities between the psychological levels of the employees and managerial styles.

Graves describes a total of seven clearly definable levels as well as additional ones that are indicated.

1. *Autistic behavior:* This involves mere survival; there is no consciousness of one's own existence. This level neither plays a role in the working world nor in management.
2. *Animistic existence:* At this level, individuals are characterized by magical thinking and superstition. Management only functions within strict limits and only if it does not contradict with superstitions and taboos. Because concepts of time, space and other dimensions are lacking, productivity is quite low. Up to a certain degree, they can be "motivated" by pure force.
3. *Awakening and fear:* There are many working individuals at this level. Because of many things that are difficult to understand, they create an orderly, predictable, consistent world in which everything is predetermined. Management will only function if clear, strict rules are set and enforced.
4. *Aggression and power:* Individuals at the fourth level believe in the power of the self. They see it as their given right to do and change things according to their will. The situation becomes critical if both management and employees are at this level. The real battle revolves more around power in the organization and less around material gains, which is why individual financial incentive systems do not always work. Graves believes that productivity is a function of the psychology of the controller and the controlled as well as certain situational factors.
5. *Socio-centric attitude:* At this level, individuals start to concern themselves less with personal and tangible matters and more with social issues. They value a pleasant working atmosphere and a comfortable work pace, which slows down output relative to the previous levels. Managers at this level concern themselves both with production and individuals. From a strategic perspective, this entails increasing employee satisfaction, which leads to increased

productivity. This is because in production, the satisfaction of social needs now is the first priority. Motivation is thus achieved via the group in which a common goal is achieved. This can lead to difficulties if excessive community thinking hinders decision making, which thereby leads to nothing being done. If the attitude is interpreted as "softened" and controlled by management, this can lead to resistance.

6. *Aggressive individualism:* At this level, individuals are no longer controlled by typical fears. They are aware of their abilities to survive. They responsibly recognize the meaningful quality and performance standards of management. They are thereby result-oriented and not sense-oriented. At the same time, they are concerned with completing a task but not how this is done. They will not be told when, where, or how a job should be done. Management is seen as assuming a merely advisory role (rather than one of strict requirements and policies), in taking on only the bare minimum of planning and organization.

7. *Pacifistic individualism:* Graves designates this level as a milder version of the sixth level. Individuals at this level are still goal-oriented and not sense-oriented; they are not, however, so "anti". They insist on an atmosphere characterized by trust and respect and wish to be fully involved in their organization as they are. They take tasks quite seriously. They value doing what is personally important to them. The suitable approach for this is acceptance management, i.e. accepting individuals for who they are, recognizing them as being competent and responsible in their field and supporting them in doing what they want. Management adapts the organization to the employees and not the other way around.

Nature of Existence	Motivational System	Value System	Appropriate Managerial System
1. Autistic	Physiological	Amoral	Close Care and Nurturing
2. Animistic	Survival	Totem and Taboo	Simple Demonstration: Force

3. Awakening	Order	Constructive	Moralistic and Prescriptive
4. Aggressive Power-Seeking	Mastery	Power	Personal, Perspective and Hard Bargaining
5. Sociocentric	Belonging	"Group-Mindedness"	Participative-Substitutive
6. Aggressive Individualistic	Self-Esteem	Personal	Goal-Setting without Prescribing Means to Goals
7. Pacifistic Individualistic	Information	Cognitive	Acceptance and Support

For Graves, the solution of the problem of the deterioration of work standards does not lie in changing individuals, but in changing the organization. Employees are not objects to be manipulated but rather humans who should be respected. In turn, they will provide good performance, thereby contributing to a high work standard.

WITH MADDEN, H.T. AND MADDEN, L.P.: THE CONGRUENT MANAGEMENT STRATEGY (1970)

In this article, along with consultants Dr Helen T. Madden and Lynn P. Madden, Graves describes congruent management strategy. They assume that striving for the best method of leadership, motivation, and management only leads to confusion and frustration and does not provide any clear results. This theory is based on recognizing the differences between individuals. They are motivated by different stimuli, for which there is no pattern.

The different existential levels are associated with preferences for certain styles of management. Individuals react based on their levels. If management principles are appropriate, they will react positively. Rejection and negative reaction can be expected in the case of an inappropriate management style.

If individuals exhibit potential for change in the case of environmental and circumstantial changes, they can reach another developmental level. This requires a change in management style so that both remain congruent.

The real task of management is therefore not to find the perfect management approach but rather to recognize the psychological differences in individuals and providing the appropriate management style.

Automatic (Beige, 1, A-N)	Only motivated by essential, regular physiological needs – hunger, sleep – strives for individually stable body function by automatic reactions. No concept of time, distance, connection and self-awareness.
Tribalistic (purple, 2, B-O)	Seeks social (tribal) stability. Explains existence in a dichotomous way – good/bad, taboo, superstition. Low self-awareness, united in the "tribe", believes that the tribal path is predetermined by nature. The task of everyday life is thus to continue this.
Egocentric (Red, 3, C-P)	Fully aware of their lonely existence. Life is like a jungle; only the strong survive. Proud, greedy, aggressive, look after themselves and then others, law of the jungle. Prove themselves through heroism – when successful, they are chosen and free to do what they want. The losers have failed or never really tried; they earn nothing and are subordinate. Open and unabashed expression of individual desires of the heroes and hidden and insincere expression of losers.
Saintly (blue, 4, D-Q)	Prescribed rules for everyone and everything. Obedience and subordination is the price for a long and secure life. The world is viewed as ordered, predictable and consistent – based on an external, often superhuman authority. All are obliged to accept the order of things and not to doubt or fight for themselves. Security comes from sacrifice and subordination.

Materialistic (Orange, 5, E-R)	The overriding concern is to control the world towards one's own goals. Exploring, discovering and questioning boundaries as well as science, rationality, efficiency and success are all means of gaining control or influence. In a cold and pragmatic matter, all tools are implemented as they fit – dishonesty, fraud and deceit are used when required. Individuals are capable of learning the skills and techniques required – the self-created individual. All things are economically based and come at a cost. But never unscrupulously because this does not pay off. Controlled expression of ambition, greed and lust – opening up gives others the chance to manipulate. It is therefore better to be discreet and not too trusting. If necessary, do it alone.
Personalistic (green, 6, F-S)	Identifying with others and one's self is central. Being liked and being with others is more important than material gains and power. Prepared to go along with the group opinion. A strong need to be accepted and the unconditional acceptance of others. Belonging to a group is highly valued – all individual values, concepts, morals and ethics come from the group and can change overnight. Any external individuals, things, or concepts have no valid claim beyond what the group permits. Group processes, consensus, majority rule and sensitivity training are valued.

Cognitive (yellow, 7, A'-N')	Interest for oneself and the world in which one lives. Information oriented, pragmatic and searches for the best solution based on current information. Values and concepts are derived from the current situation. Motivation comes from within – seeks a sense of personal competence. Those who possess information about the current situation should lead. If the situation changes, so should the leadership – rotating leadership. No longer motivated by fear of survival, fear of God, material wealth, fear of social rejection – discreet awareness of surviving on one's own ability, come what may. Free from the constraints and fears of the previous levels. A truly cooperative individual who recognizes the interdependence of all things and has no need for destructive, individual competition. Despite all of this, capable of ruthlessness when the situation requires.
Experientialistic (turquoise 8, B'-O')	Through personal experience, these individuals show that – no matter how much information is available – not everything can be understood. Astonishment, awe, reverence, gratitude, unity and simplicity are appreciated. Reality can be experienced, but one can never be certain about it. There is an atmosphere of trust and respect. Stand up against constraints and limitations on a quiet and personal manner – never in a showcasing manner. Avoid relationships in which others try to dominate – do not like to dominate others but rather specify a clear direction insofar as it is necessary.

The individual is unique and complex and is formed in layers, level by level, based on an A-N (1 / beige) core. These are not uniform but rather "wrinkled". They vary in thickness from negligible to substantial. They are also flexible and adapt dynamically.

Description of the levels:

1) Automatic (beige, A-N) – nurturing:

The only appropriate management style at this level is nurturing. Otherwise, the subordinates will perish. However, this level does not play a role in the US working world.

2) Tribalistic (purple, 2, B-O) – friendly parent:

Productive effort can only be expected from individuals at this level if the work contradicts neither taboos nor superstitions. Because their world is so full of these, work is often only occasional and sporadic. Managers must accept the individual lifestyle and create a model that takes their wishes into account. Employees at this level must especially be isolated from group members who do not accept their lifestyle, do not take their taboos seriously or have competing lifestyles and/or taboos. Concepts of time, space, quantity, material and life are unfortunately quite limited and productivity is limited because of industrial thinking. They require tangible, immediate supervision. In general, they find the working world to be unbelievably scary and actively avoid it as far as possible. However, if they are managed well, they work rigorously and persistently. They tend to flee from management. Sabotage and disturbances are not expected from them. However, if they are forced to work, they will attempt to dispel the apparent evil.

3) Egocentric (red, 3, C-P) – tough-paternalistic

The third level plays a larger role in the working world. Employees at this level know how they are supposed to do their job and display their pride and knowledge (regardless of the required skills, level of education and knowledge). They need to feel free to come and go as they please. The required management style is tough-paternalistic. The two-fold message to the employees is that the manager (1) can do the job better than them and (2) nevertheless respects their abilities and gives them permission to do the job. By strictly assigning tasks, the manager provides sufficient detailed information about the desired end result, the limits of free disposition and the dead line. The manager then refrains from intervening unless asked to do so. However, the manager does not display blind faith as he or she would be perceived as weak and taken advantage of. Trust is based on performance. The manager needs to estimate how long employees have to demonstrate their competence without creating risks or incurring costs. At the end of this period, the performance is evaluated and a decision is made. In the case of good performance, the employee is certified for this area. In the case of poor performance, the employee is either assigned a more suitable task or dismissed. To gain advanced skills, the employee starts an apprenticeship with a master, without a special training or time program. Mismanagement may arise from an overly restrictive, authoritarian management style. Individuals at this level perceive this as a direct attack to their pride and competence. As a result, they may choose to resign from the organization. This resignation is often violent and directed to the corresponding source of anger. Egocentric individuals will directly express their frustration and personal hate without thinking about the cost of this behavior. If a direct resignation is not possible, the manager will feel the maliciousness of the employee. Mismanagement may also occur if the manager does not appear to be a competent leader, thereby losing respect and acceptance. Employees will do as they please or leave the organization because they do not wish to work for such a person.

4) Saintly (blue, 4, D-Q) – authoritarian

Employees at this level react to an authoritarian management style whereby they know and accept their subordinate roles. For them, the task of the manager is to establish routine, to structure tasks, to define rules, to demonstrate and to represent the organization. This subordination provides them with the necessary security. This level is especially important for entrepreneurs and for government leaders because a large proportion of the workforce responds to this. Administrative activities, especially in a large organization, are especially attractive to them. If the organization introduces job enrichment, employees at this level feel threatened and perceive their employers as "evil". Some of them will prefer to transfer to a "good" organization. At this level, mismanagement entails not clearly specifying orientation and structure. For employees at the blue level (4,

D-Q), democratic, non-authoritarian management leads to physical illness and withdrawal, disruptions in life and corporate morale and a decline in productivity. This may result in neurotic or psychotic behavior, unconscious sabotage of performance and the perception that the manager is not doing his or her job.

5) Materialistic (orange, 5, E-R) – bargaining

This existential level is well known in management because it is a substantial component. Employees expect a reward for their services. High flexibility and the opportunity to be initiative are important criteria for a job. Rules have no inherent sanctity and can be circumnavigated and interpreted according to the situation. For this level, the appropriate style of management is bargaining. The employee and manager can negotiate in a direct and open manner. To lead individuals at this level, a manager requires three things: (1) rewards, (2) sanctions, and (3) defined boundaries with leeway. Organizational goals and targets are disclosed by the manager. Employees expect to be rewarded for their achievements. This plays a large role in their motivation. Rewards must therefore always be attractive to the employees and adjusted if necessary. Employees can move freely within the specified limits. However, there are clear sanctions for overstepping these limits. After negotiation, materialistic employees work diligently to achieve the discussed goals. The employees essentially manage themselves; supervision is only required to ensure that the boundaries are observed. At this level, there are essentially two forms of mismanagement. The first and most frequent happens when the rewards are not worth the effort. In most cases, this leads to the employees leaving the organization. The loss of hard-working, dynamic and innovative employees who perform well when properly managed can be highly devastating to the organization. The second form of mismanagement involves not setting limits and not setting or enforcing sanctions. Orange (5, E-R) employees will then become virtual or actual managers.

6) Personalistic (green, 6, F-S) – group process.

Employees at this level are more concerned with social matters than material ones. The work pace decreases because employees seek acceptance and a comfortable atmosphere. The appropriate style of management is the group process. The manager should be open towards the group and will become a member of the group himself, with the same "rights" as anyone else to introduce things to occupy the group and thereby act in a truly open, non-directive and participatory manner. Management is a participatory group process i.e. making suggestions within the group on one hand and specifying the direction required by the organization on the other. This will not, however, increase human effort unless the group itself creates the pressure. The number of employees at this level is highest in today's organizations and will continue to increase. The negative consequences of applying inappropriate management styles for this level are becoming more and more apparent.

There are two basic forms of mismanagement for the personalistic level. The first and currently most common one is the use of a non-participatory style of management. Managers who are not seen as part of the group do not have the right to manage. At best, they will be ignored. In the worst-case scenario, they will be viewed in a negative light and dealt with at the discretion of the group. The increasing number of individuals at this level is often viewed as a form of softening. If this development is met with direct, authoritarian management, it will have negative consequences. These can range from passive resistance accompanied by a decline in productivity to a complete paralysis of the organization. Those who are not part of the group have no rights and will be quickly excluded. The second form of mismanagement involves unconditionally connecting the manager to the group without the substitutive element of leadership. Management will thus lose its function and authority and the group will respond at its own discretion. The group itself will become the management.

7) Cognitive (yellow, 7, A'-N') – facilitation

An employee at this level absolutely agrees that management should set sensible performance standards with respect to quality and quantity and is thereby result-oriented and not means-oriented. That is why they only follow the standard operating procedures if and to the extent that they are valid. Individuals at the cognitive level feel that those with the greatest knowledge should lead – and who knows better than the acting person? The appropriate style of management is thereby process facilitation and involves recognizing the competence of the acting person. Process facilitating management often requires an open relationship between the manager and the employee i.e. all information, goals, resources and limitations are discussed. If a cognitive employee accepts a task, the manager is responsible for providing the necessary support. However, if an employee declines the task, the manager should facilitate finding a more appropriate task in another department or organization. This level is threatening for many managers; it can be difficult to accept the role as process facilitator. Mismanagement arises from not being able to assume this type of management. Employees can respond in one of three ways: (1) they see a possibility for change and try to change the situation from within the organization; (2) they see no possibility for change, subordinate themselves and work according to the specifications; (3) they leave the organization and seek out a suitable alternative. Malicious or destructive behavior should not be expected in any of these cases. Management is often not aware of anything negative and is thus surprised when employees chose to leave the enterprise.

8) Experientialistic (turquoise 8, B'-O') – facilitation

Individuals at this level insist on a trusting and respectful atmosphere and expect to be integrated into the organization. They primarily focus on resisting constraints and limitations, albeit to a lesser extent than individuals at the cognitive level do. They take their work quite seriously and occupy themselves with what they personally want to do. It is also important to take their competence and responsibility seriously and approach them with process facilitation and acceptance management. It makes no sense to place the interests of the employees below those of the organization. Instead, the organization must adapt to the employees via management. Here, mismanagement results in disorganized work and mediocre performance until changes are made to management.

Management strategy – what is to be done?

In the direct relationship between the manager and employee (one-on-one), the application of a congruent management style is fairly clear and straightforward. However, managers must normally deal with entire working groups consisting of individuals at different levels. The congruent management strategy consists of the following phases:

1. *Introduction (reintroduction):* The manager must (re)introduce the original management style. Each employee must be given the possibility of viewing the role of the manager as positive, without decreasing the productivity of the group.
2. *Analysis:* Through stimulus-response situations, the manager collects information about the operant levels of the employees in professional situations.
3. *Congruence:* With the help of this information, the manager switches from the original management style to a congruent style for each individual employee (one-on-one). This is done over a longer period of time.
4. *Growth:* In the existing manager-employee relationship, the manager introduces elements that enable individual growth.

The key to implementing this strategy is the original management style, a universally accepted form of management.

The original universal style of management

The original style of management is polite, open and authoritarian (POA). It is appropriate for all levels except for beige (1, A-N) and purple (2, B-O), which, according to Graves, only play a negligible role in the working world. The principles are as follows:

- *Polite:* non-threatening, tough but fair, no favorites, civilized and cultivated.
- *Open:* inviting genuine participation; willing to listen and respond positively to information; stimulate discussions; seek ideas, suggestions, comments and criticism from all parties; support employees in meeting the needs of the organization.
- *Authoritarian:* clearly communicating that the manager has the final decision; providing a general program to be carried out if there are no other suggestions, specifying individual positions and those of the department; acting as a competent and capable manager.

This is the only universal style of management that is accepted by all levels. It is realistic, situative and information-oriented. This will naturally emerge from cognitive individuals (yellow, 7, A'-N').

Analysis, congruence and growth

In the original management style, the manager assigns individual tasks that match the work to date. The analysis process continues until the manager has collected enough information to initiate change toward a congruent management style.

This gradual development has several advantages e.g. higher productivity of the group as a result of better individual performance and a better climate in the organization. In addition, there is a chance of reaching higher existential levels. This necessitates the joining of three aspects: (1) the congruence of management style and the level of the employees must be maintained so that the relationship will also be maintained; (2) dissonance is brought into the situation and values, perceptions and behaviors are questioned; (3) a behavioral model of the next level is presented. Here, the manager always pays attention to the degree of rejection or acceptance on the part of the employee and adjusts his or her style of management accordingly. If the values, perceptions and behaviors of the next level have already been partially accepted, the positive phase of growth has begun.

Positive effects are only expected when all steps of the process have been implemented.

Aspects of growth management

LEVEL	DISSONANCE MODEL NATURE	NEGATIVE INFORMATION
Egocentric (red, 3, C-P)	First, immediate rewards come from the willingness to accept regulations, structure and order. Order later provides its own reward – security	Increases aggressive behavior, misuse of rewards (normally increased responsibility), making victims of the weak
Saintly (blue, 4, D-Q)	Individual obligations can best be fulfilled through the willingness to be flexible – violation of order. The reward later results from success and not from submission	Increased use of order in personally-defensive manner – increased inflexibility
Materialistic (Orange 5, E-R)	Organize almost any situation in such a way that interaction with others (as individual human beings) is necessary in order to achieve goals. Choose others that cannot be bought, intimidated, or manipulated but who react positively when they are treated with humanity. Require openness in interaction	Avoid turning away from those situations requiring open interaction. Obsessive-compulsive tendency to manipulate things
Personalistic (green, 6, F-S)	Attempts to incorporate the reality of the external world into their group perspective. Strengthening the group concept by everything that comes from the outside	Not prepared to look outside the box – including group ranks and the denial of reality – increased inward orientation
Cognitive (yellow, 7, A'-N')	Creation of all information for all situations – completely open books. Encouraging the inclusion of all things – the broad view	Biased selection of information – establishing perceptual filters

On the one hand, the polite, open, authoritarian style is accepted by all and is therefore optimally suited as an entry or re-entry. On the other hand, this can always be used as a withdrawal option, should something go wrong during the analysis. In any situation, this can be used with mixed groups. There is a risk of switching to an individual, level-specific style, which results in the integration of some and the exclusion of others. For those at the cognitive level (yellow, 7, A'-N'), this style naturally feels comfortable and should be the easiest to implement. There are, however, situations, in which managers who react at other levels are more successful.

The central point is finding and applying a management style that is congruent to each employee and not imposing a preferred style on anybody. Change can only be successful if it is valued.

THE LEVELS OF HUMAN EXISTENCE AND THEIR RELATION TO WELFARE PROBLEMS (1970)

In this lecture, Graves speaks of the relationship between existential levels and the problem of social assistance. He cites five different case studies of families from each of the first five existential levels and notes that social assistance does not provide adequate support in any of them. There does not seem to be any appropriate concept for that humans – and their problems – grow and develop.

The woman in the first case is at the first existential level (beige, A-N). She has little energy and is incapable of caring for herself. She requires basic, concrete assistance from individuals so that she can slowly develop towards the second existential level.

The family in the second case is at the second existential level (purple, B-O). Their lives are determined by magic and superstition. Their concepts of space and time are severely limited. They also require concepts in their life they can connect to, e.g. mobile medical care.

In the third case, Graves describes an encounter with an angry man at the third existential level (red, C-P). This level poses a great challenge for social assistance because for these individuals, the world is of full of anger and mistrust. They are highly demanding and impatient and thus require rapid and direct processes and immediately available contacts.

The woman in the fourth case, a widow with two young children, is at the fourth existential level (blue D-Q) in a world full of dependence and authority at every step. She requires constant guidance and support in order to ensure that she does the right thing.

The Williams family in case five is at the fifth existential level (orange, E-R) and was independent and self-sufficient until their foundation got unsteady and they were suddenly entitled to receive assistance. In order to develop their independence, they require property protection, a guaranteed income and the possibility of receiving a loan.

Graves believes that successful social assistance (in terms of concepts and administrative implementation) must be tailored to the respective levels of the clients. These groups must first be identified in order to determine the appropriate careers, individuals and methods, which are congruent to the target groups. Crises and confrontation should be viewed as a sign of success rather than failure.

HOW SHOULD WHO LEAD WHOM TO DO WHAT? (1971–72)

Both research and experience show that (1) managers that succeed in one situation may fail miserably in another, (2) good results from one group cannot always be replicated in another, and (3) there is no way of obtaining key information on which appropriate management can be based. This paper thus aims to find it and thereby introduce more clarity to the many specifics of management situations.

Graves cites cybernetics (the science of controlling machines, living organisms and social organizations, *author's note*), which has a substantial influence on management but are inadequately implemented in many places. The title "How Should Who Lead Whom To Do What?" presents a systemic problem. Managers thus require a basic understanding of how a system works. According to cybernetics, effective management in various situations succeeds in part by knowing certain relationships between at least four work sub-systems. These are (1) the sub-system of the strategies, practices and processes dealing with the philosophy and practice of management; (2) the sub-system of executives (e.g. managers and administrators) and its system of beliefs, which is reflected in its behavior; (3) the psychological sub-system of the managed individuals and their values and beliefs as well as how they would like to be managed and how they assess and react to management; and (4) the sub-system of the work that needs to be done and that is assigned to the employee by the manager. These are all related to each other and are in turn situated within a larger system with which they are also related. If only one sub-system is uncoordinated with another or with the entire system, the entire system suffers. In order to be able to expect maximum performance, the entire management situation must be congruent.

Incongruence has a negative influence on managers, employees and work-related performance. Graves finds the question of how to motivate employees to be ridiculous. This is because he believes that everyone is motivated as long as he or she is alive. It is a question of which method is right for whom. Every complete switch of a motivational strategy would result in some coping better and others coping worse or not at all. There is no method for making everyone happy; there is no optimum solution. This applies to both managers and employees.

Effective management therefore results from the fact that (1) different kinds of work are organized in a different manner, (2) namely in a way that those individuals do the work, that are psychologically compatible with it (in relationship to variety, security vs. risk and strict vs. relaxed leadership), 3) the natural leadership style of the manager is a fit for the employees and tasks and 4) the manager's introduced methods fit his management style, the work and the people doing the work. Applied to the existential levels, this means that for every level, there are appropriate or congruent modes of operation, structures and management styles. Here, it is important to differentiate between individuals with an open personality and those with a closed one i.e. those who have remained at a particular level and will continue to do so. While the former often prefer the management style of the next level and experience this as congruent, this is unthinkable for the latter. For the latter, the congruent style is the one of his or her own level. It may happen, for example, that in one organization, sections A, B and C do not work efficiently towards the production of product X because the teams each consist of individuals from three different existential levels. In that case, a reallocation to the team managers or a reorganization of the employees may be one solution for ensuring that management style, tasks and employees fit together.

Levels of Existence	Style of Management
1. A-N: automatic	1. A-N: reactive
2. B-O: tribalistic	2. B-O: traditionalistic
3. C-P: egocentric	3. C-P: exploitative
4. D-Q: saintly	4. D-Q: paternalistic
5. E-R: materialistic	5. E-R: consultative
6. F-S: sociocentric	6. F-S: participative
7. G-T: cognitive	7. G-T: facilitative
8. H-U: experientalistic	8. H-U: systemic

LEVELS OF EXISTENCE RELATED TO LEARNING SYSTEMS (1971)

In this article, Graves discusses the methodological and philosophical problems involved in the planning and creating of learning systems. He first criticizes the manner in which most existing programs function. There is usually an authority that prescribes what is to be learned at a particular time and how. Graves does not think much of this. He believes that there are great differences in the manner in which individuals learn and how they are motivated to learn. These depend on their existential levels. Similarly, they require different structures, stimuli and methods of learning that are congruent with the respective level. Graves describes the individual levels in detail.

At the beige level (1, A-N), individuals are only motivated by stimuli that directly meet their physiological needs. They adapt through the process of habituation. At this level, learning does not take place in the sense of lasting pattern changes. Thus, the development of special learning systems is not needed here.

At the purple level (2, B-O), learning takes place according to the principles of classical conditioning. This type of learning takes place when rapid changes of external stimuli meet with innate reflexes. However, this is an inconvenient method for learning. It is mostly known from the experiments with Pavlovian dogs.

Things are different at the red level (3, C-P) because learning takes place according to the trial-and-error method and operant conditioning i.e. the reward system (mostly known from B.F. Skinner). Desirable actions must be rewarded immediately and in a manner attractive to the learner in order to consolidate them. This reduces the tension present in the operating condition.

At the blue level (4, D-Q), individuals are particularly sensitive to punishment. Their motivation lies in avoiding aversive stimulation. In order to motivate individuals at this level, the appropriate time and type of punishment must be determined in order to optimally integrate them into the learning system. The learning method of O. Hobart Mowrer is in line with this.

If the orange level (5, E-R) is dominant, latent stimulus-response learning should be used. What motivates people on this level is to challenge and to change ideal issues as well as the extent to which the result corresponds to the expectations. Individuals at this level can expect the corresponding reward as long as the learning activity is self-controlled and not regulated by knowledgeable authorities. At this level, the cornerstones are learning through one's own effort, the presence of low risk, the individual experience and great variety in learning events. The work of E. C. Tolman and J. B. Rotter is in line with this.

At the green level (6, F-S), learning takes place through observing and modelling. Knowledge and potential behavior is being acquired individually, without receiving any direct external reinforcement for one's own actions. In this case, the consequences that lead to a certain behavior in others will be observed. This type of learning is closely connected to the work of Bandura and Walters.

For Graves, the main differences lie less in what individuals think or in the information they process, but more in how they actually do that. Individuals at the purple level (2, B-O) thus think in an autistic (withdrawn) and syncretic (forming, blended) manner. Conversely, individuals at the red level (3, C-P) think in an egocentric, impulsive and hedonistic manner, which is focused on immediate pleasure and not considering the consequences for others. Individuals at the blue level (4, D-Q) think in an authoritarian, rigid, moralizing, black-and-white manner and learning entails the regurgitation of facts. At the orange level (5, E-R), situative and relative thinking comes into play. Even if there are several answers to a question, there is always one best answer. Rational understanding in an impersonal, objective and detached manner dominates, whereby the entire process is viewed as a game with exact rules, which enable one to win. In addition, they like to divide things and reassemble them to form their own concepts. This is different from the green level (6, F-S), because here the focus is on personal relevance. Perception and sensation are more important than understanding things. At the yellow level (7, A'-N'), knowledge always exists in certain contexts. Different points of view can be accepted and co-exist. For them, the teacher's task is to provide problems and to indicate ways of recognizing, to then accept the individual solution or conclusion of each one.

It is thus important to recognize the diversity and variety of learning and provide the corresponding environment, methods and materials in order to optimally promote each one individually.

Clare W. Graves

HUMAN NATURE PREPARES FOR A MOMENTOUS LEAP (1974)

Graves' 20 years of research led him to the conclusion that human values are not fixed and that humans do not live according to one certain set of values. Rather, the individual learns that a certain way of life and the associated values make sense for one period of his or her development, however, not necessarily for a later one. Graves' data suggest that the nature of man is an open, constantly evolving system, which jumps from one stable system to the next in a hierarchical order. In short, the psychology of the mature human being is an unfolding, emerging, oscillating and spiraling process. If life conditions change, older, lower-ranking and less complex systems are thereby subordinated to newer, higher-ranking, more complex biopsychosocial systems. These systems switch back and forth between the focus on the external world and the attempts to change it and the focus on the inner world and the attempts to come into harmony with it and adjust it to the given life conditions. Individuals inherently possess all aspects of the level at which they are situated. Their feelings, ethics, values, motivation, learning systems, beliefs and concept of mental health and physical illnesses (and their treatments) as well as their preferences for management styles, notions of education and political systems all match this state. In some cases, individuals are not capable (e.g. for genetic reasons) to develop to the next existential level when their life conditions change. They instead stabilize at one level or a particular constellation of levels. An individual can positively or negatively display behavior typical of a level. Regression to a previous level is also possible. An adult generally lives in a potentially open system of needs, values and expectations but often remains in an apparently closed system.

In relation to the current US society, Graves predicts an increased emergence of the sixth personalistic level (F-S, green) e.g. in the form of yoga, self-help groups and participatory forms of decision making in management. Here, the individual is concerned with achieving inner harmony and harmony with others. This is viewed as the ultimate goal in life. This shortsighted mind-set is typical for individuals at all levels, as long as they remain trapped inside.

The "generation gap" is much more a conflict of values between the D-Q (4, blue), E-R (5, orange) and F-S (6, green) levels. For example, it is difficult for parents at the fifth level (E-R, orange) to understand why their children (6, F-S, green) reject their ideas of material wealth, competition and career. This is instead perceived as being weak or lazy. The passive resistance and civil disobedience displayed by the F-S youth (6, green) resulted in them being labeled as "anarchists" because they oppose existing rules and systems without providing a comprehensible alternative. In large parts of society, this creates fear of the decay of typical American values. The attitude towards technology is also subject to major change. Driven by people at the fifth level (E-R, orange) and an important part of progress, they are rejected as an instrument of conquest by individuals at the sixth level (F-S, green). They are more strongly oriented toward nature and reject its exploitation for material growth. Nevertheless, what will happen if the majority of humanity arrives at this harmonic level? Who will care for daily needs and vital technologies? At a certain point, this does not end well. New problems in the form of energy, ecological and population crises as well as growth limitation will produce great pressure for change, thus resulting in a leap to the first level of being (7, A'-N', yellow).

A leap from one level to the next is comparable with basic phenomena of quantum physics and neurophysiology i.e. it is derived from the same laws of hierarchical organization. Individuals must resolve hierarchical existential problems, which leads to the release of energy and gives rise to new problems. Dynamic, higher-order neurological systems are thereby biochemically activated. Human growth is mostly inhibited by external circumstances such as poverty, helplessness and social rejection. The full expression of one's level is therefore usually impossible. However, in order to arrive at the next level up, the limits of the current value system must be completely experienced. The step to the next level is made possible by recognizing that newly arising problems cannot be solved using the current value system. The available coping mechanisms become insufficient. Individuals at the fifth level (E-R, orange) must first gain power over nature in order to recognize that beyond the problem of power is the problem of knowing one's self (6, F-S, green). The E-R level (5, orange) also resulted from a protest against self-sacrifice and the deference of one's interests (4, D-Q, blue). The development from C-P (3, red) to D-Q (4, blue) resulted from a need for rules and security, to reduce the anger people attracted to each other.

The time at a particular level can be divided into three phases: First, in the (1) embryonic phase, those values required to solve new existential problems are identified in order to apply these in the (2) implementation phase to solve the problems, and ultimately in (3) the phase of collapse that follows the successful solution. An additional phase is the recognition of new values, which often represent an antithesis to the previous ones and mark the final collapse of the previous social or individual basis.

Finally, Graves notes that the time spent at a particular level decreases with the higher levels. From an evolutionary point of view, individuals spent a long time at the lower existential levels, while the upper levels constitute a development of the last few decades.

Graves describes three possibilities for future development. First of all, we could continue to regress further as a result of various catastrophes that arise from the failure to stabilize the world. Second, stabilization at the blue (4, D-Q), orange (5, E-R), and green (6, F-S) complex could occur, also with precarious downsides: tyrannical, manipulative governments masked by humanitarian-like, ambiguous and moral rationalizations. The third possibility would be continued development to yellow (7, A'-N'), which would lead to a very different world with another way of thinking. Unbridled self-expression and self-indulgence would no longer play a role, because the theme here is that all life can exist. There is a new form of authority that is not God-given or self-serving but rather based on knowledge and necessity. This involves restoring the balance of earth so that sustainable living is possible. Topics such as renewable resources with respect to energy and clothing as well as emission-free transportation play a large role here and advanced technologies are implemented. Fear and coercion and magical-mystical ideas are outdated, paradoxes accepted and contradictions can co-exist. We once again know how to appreciate small pleasures, give ourselves the satisfaction to lead happy lives and no longer waste time on unnecessary things. Detached and untouched by social realities, we are still aware of our existence. Without placing a high value on our own egos, we are concerned with the correctness of our existence. They enjoy the best of everything without being dependent on it. There is decentralization at the level of organizations. Only essential work is performed, although the nature, structure, quantity, space, time and reason have changed. This will also have a major impact on our education. Rather than narrow, predetermined systems, everyone will be encouraged to make full use of his or her value systems and a more natural growth process, free of any constraints, will evolve. Equal access to a high-quality life would be self-evident. Pronounced wealth or poverty would be inappropriate because the balance sought for would not be maintained. Quality will replace quantity as a standard. Because the system and development are open, Graves can imagine that additional levels will arise in the future, although these cannot yet be described. However, the levels of the second tier can be predicted by reversing the values of a level at the first rank and transferring them to a higher form of complexity.

Movement through the individual levels can be described as follows:

Reactive values (beige, 1, A-N): Pure response to environmental conditions to ensure one's own survival, but without self-awareness.

Traditionalistic values (purple, 2, B-O): The main value at this level is security, the elementary means of tradition. Dominated by tribal traditions, individuals become social. They value what ancestors and elders have prescribed. If these values are ever inappropriate for younger individuals, boredom or challenges will lead to attacking this establishment and thereby a development towards red (3, C-P).

Exploitative values (red, 3, C-P): At this level, one recognizes oneself as a separate being and begins to place one's survival and advancement at the forefront. People do not want to be dominated but rather desire control over their existence. By responding to one's impact on the world in the form of reward or punishment, this is evaluated as a success or failure. Many attempt to be successful, but only a few achieve this goal. The stronger prevail; there are heroes and losers. However, if both winners and losers of this system question the explanation of their fate (i.e. the "why" question), a new existential problem arises. Belief in a given system arises, thereby resulting in the development towards blue (D-Q).

Sacrificial values (blue, 4, D-Q): The aim here is to give up earthly desires in order to later obtain everlasting peace. Important values include renunciation, self-discipline, modesty and piety. One's own role and position in life is accepted and not questioned. Rules are black and white, life is a serious matter and only non-independent fun is permitted. There is an ultimate authority, which sets the rules. At some point, some begin to doubt these values and rules and yearn for pleasure in their present lives. This starts development towards orange (5, E-R). For some, this development is exciting and refreshing. For others, who maintain the blue point of view, this is a human depravity.

Materialistic values (orange, 5, E-R): At this level, individuals strive towards independence because they view life as limited due to the lack of control over their environment. They rationally and objectively explore the world. However, they are careful not to provoke the wrath of others. Materialism is the standard. This mode of existence is described as pragmatic, scientific and benefit-oriented. Measurability, feasibility of the technology, target and profit orientation and entrepreneurial thinking are the typical characteristics of orange (5, E-R). Prosperity, process and knowledge are created, thereby improving living conditions. However, just as earthly existential problems appear to have been solved, new existential problems arise. There is a lack of belonging and connections because up until now, these individuals had been attempting to achieve their goals alone.

Personalistic values (green, 6, F-S): Green also values authority, although it is that of contemporaries. Matters are determined by the peer group, the group to which one belongs. Those at this level desire to be connected with valued individuals and their feelings. Communication, majority rule, persuasion over force, sensitivity over objectivity, taste over wealth, and people over things are all characteristics of the green world. Getting along is more important than overtaking others; cooperation is valued over competition.

Existential values (yellow, 7, A'-N'): Individuals at this level recognize themselves and their world in full clarity and encounter an unsatisfactory image. They seek ways and possibilities of escaping the parasitic exploitation of their world in order to achieve true self-esteem and a solid basis. They can create this basis though the yellow value system, which is deeply rooted in knowledge and cosmic reality. Behavior is correct if it is based on the best possible evidence. What was right yesterday is not necessarily appropriate today. The current reality is the deciding factor. The theme of this level is expressing one's self in such a way that all living beings may continue to exist. The yellow value system is no longer fixated on satisfying selfish interests. Instead, the magnificence of existence is recognized as well as the desire to obtain it.

In order to reach a higher existential level, the following is required: (1) the necessary potential in the brain, (2) the solution to the existential problem of the previous level, (3) dissonance or a collapse in solving the current existential problem i.e. a crisis, (4) insight, (5) the overcoming of limitations, and (6) the consolidation of the new system.

SUMMARY STATEMENT: THE EMERGENT, CYCLICAL, DOUBLE-HELIX MODEL OF THE ADULT HUMAN BIOPSYCHOSOCIAL SYSTEMS (1981)

The emergent, cyclical, double-helix model describes, explains and suggests possibilities for dealing with the biopsychosocial development of *homo sapiens* as well as individuals and relatively homogeneous groups. According to the theory:

1. The biopsychosocial development of humans arises from the interacting forces of a double helix that consists of environmental and social determinants (existential problems of life) and the neuropsychological features of the organism (neuropsychological features of life).

2) The biopsychosocial development of the mature human is an unfolding, emerging, oscillating and spiraling process. Older, lower-ranking and less complex systems are thereby subordinated to newer, higher-ranking, more complex biopsychosocial systems.
3) These systems switch between the focus on the external world and the attempts to change this (dominance of the left cerebral hemisphere) and the focus on the inner world and the attempts to come into harmony with it (dominance of the right cerebral hemisphere) with the aim and possibility of alternately changing each part of the system to the next system.
4) Individuals tend to adjust their biopsychosocial being if they change their life conditions.
5) Individuals inherently possess all aspects of the level at which they are situated. Their feelings, motivation, concept of physical illnesses and values as well as their preference for certain managerial and educational concepts all match this condition.
6) In some cases, individuals are not capable (e.g. for genetic reasons) of developing to the next existential level if their life conditions change.
7) Individuals can stabilize themselves at one level or a certain constellation of levels.
8) An individual can positively or negatively display behavior typical of a level.
9) Under certain circumstances, an individual can regress to a lower existential level.
10) Because of specific organizational or environmental premises, a person will settle in a relatively closed system instead of a more open state of development.
11) Human development is comparable with a symphony, which begins with the simplest form of themes and melodies and continues to develop towards virtually infinite variations. These life themes will change once individuals have resolved current existential problems. This in turn results in the creation of new existential problems.
12) At this point in time, the modern technological nations are in the process of finalizing the original approach of the green level (6,

F-S). The US is beginning with the first topic of the second round: the yellow level (7, A'-N'). The first existential spiral has been completed and a completely new set of survival problems has arisen. Individuals at this level are seriously thinking about the mutual dependencies of existences and no longer about individual, independent existence. Thus begins the second spiral of existence, the level system of being.
13) Any upward movement in the existential levels is accompanied by an enlargement of the conceptual space of the individual.
14) To date, nine different conditions have emerged.

At the first subsistential level (beige, A-N), the autistic existential condition, the theme is expressing oneself like other species and fulfilling one's necessary recurrent physical needs. Concepts of space and time are quite limited and there is no awareness of one's self. Concepts of organization and management do not yet exist.

At the second subsistential level (purple, B-O), the animistic existential condition, the theme is sacrificing one's own needs in order to satisfy the elders. This arises from a lack of security e.g. in relation to important resources such as food or water supplies. These problems (B) activate the corresponding neuropsychological system (O) which reacts to the need to avoid pain, hunger, cold and danger and recognizes and reacts to threatening situations. Magical/mystical thinking, totems and taboos determine the world and individuals live in tribal cultures. Everything is predetermined; the nature of things cannot be changed.

At the third subsistential level (red, C-P), the egocentric existential condition, the theme is expressing oneself without considering others so that one escapes the torment of unbearable shame. This level is reached when the C problems of existence arise after relative security has been achieved. Boredom is the reason why risk-taking and new concepts of space and chronological time arise. For the first time, individuals demarcate themselves from their environment and others. This results in uninhibited, amoral and egocentric behavior. Each individual wishes to win, but only the strong will prevail. They divide individuals into three classes: (1) the strong, chosen and proactive, (2) the motivated but yet not proactive and (3) the weak and lazy who need and want leadership. At the organizational level, the chosen ones use the masses in order to achieve their goals, which is why this form of management is designated as exploitative. The chosen few see their doing as completely justified and dictate where to go as well as who must do what and how. At this level, learning takes place through operant conditioning as well as trial and error with a high risk. At this level, few are very successful, some are moderately so and many not at all.

At the fourth subsistential level (blue, D-Q), the absolutist existential condition, the theme is sacrificing one's own needs in order to be rewarded in the future. This level arises when confrontation with misery, which results from the limited degree of success and high degree of failure, leads to individual concern with the meaning of life. At this level, the answer lies in a higher power, in God, or in the design of nature. This higher power may not be questioned. There is only one right way of doing things. The absolutist thinking only allows black or white, good or bad, friend or enemy. There are pre-defined roles and strict hierarchical systems. A change of position is viewed as a weakness. This level brings out paternalistic or benevolent-autocratic management.

At the fifth subsistential level (orange, E-R), the diverse existential condition, the theme is expressing one's self in order to fulfil one's needs, albeit it in a calculated manner without awaking the anger of others. The higher power is no longer sufficient to solve problems or to establish security and order. Expressing oneself is necessary in order to carry out what the higher power has created but not controlled. At this level, there are several different ways; however, only one of them is considered the correct one. Hypothetico-deductive (conclusion of a general theory to special individual findings, *author's note*) and mechanistic (only recognizing mechanic causes, *author's note*) thinking predominates and displaces the moral predetermination of the previous levels. It is important to analyze things and understand how they can be changed and not why something is the way it is. What is right must be determined through extensive investigation. Specialization, simplification, objective qualification criteria and evaluation as well as the replaceability of parts are typical of management at this level. Productivity and increased profits are important goals.

At the sixth subsistential level (green, F-S), the relativistic existential condition, the theme is sacrificing oneself so that all may benefit. Those who had profited from the previous system sense the growing antipathy of the less successful. Over time, the need arises to be liked and to share the fruits of success. The individuality of the others is recognized just as one's own. Society moves to the forefront and goal orientation shifts towards the group. This involves joint decisions and experiences. Participatory management arises and consensus becomes the preferred form of decision. All voices are heard and decisions are only made when all participants are in agreement. Being accepted by others is more important than getting one's way. Long-term, qualitative goals are more important than short-term, quantitative goals. At the same time, it is clear who does and does not belong to the group. Outsiders are excluded; the advancement of one's own group is important. Management and employees have a great deal of mutual trust.

At the first level of being (yellow, A'-N'), the systemic existential condition, the theme is expressing one's self in order to fulfil one's needs in a way that all can benefit and never at the cost of others. This marks the beginning of systematic thinking. The previous coping system is combined with the new one, which expands the capacity of conceptual thinking to a large extent. This represents the largest developmental step. Individuals at this level have shared objectives but are not ambitious. Compulsiveness and anxiety disappear. There are worries and concerns, but these are not bothersome or threatening. Individuals approach things intellectually rather than emotionally. There are many possibilities, but nothing is compulsory. Successes are gratifying, but if something does not work out, this is also acceptable. Different opinions and interpretations can be accepted and co-exist. This involves determining which type of thinking is appropriate in a certain context and at a certain time. Authority and leadership are situational and based on the insight of who possesses the relevant competencies and information to overcome the current challenges. Management is facilitative, the competence of the employees is recognized and leadership is kept to a minimum. It is assumed that individuals have different abilities and needs. Employees are productive when they can apply their abilities and when their needs are fulfilled. Management is responsible for creating these opportunities. The organization adapts to the employees via management and not vice versa.

The table shows how human biopsychosocial development has developed over the last 40,000 years. The various layers each represent a Gravesian existential level. Starting with the purple level (2, B-O), he cites concrete years, which become more precise with each increasing level. The date of origin is the year 1977.

AN	n/a
BO	40.000 years ago
CP	10.000 years ago
DQ	4.000 years ago
ER	1.400 years ago
FS	80 years ago
A'N'	30 years ago
B'O'	15 years ago

In an illustration of his model, Graves shows first- and second order existential problems on the x-axis, while first and second order coping systems are shown on the y-axis. Two wave-like lines show alternating spurt and plateau stages in development. The dashed line represents any existential level in which the focus is on the external world and the attempt to master this. According to Graves, this was accompanied by left-hemisphere control and dominance at the neurological level. For the solid line, the right hemisphere is dominant. It represents all existence levels in which the focus is on the internal being and the attempt to come to peace with it. The complexity increases from level to level, which is why the systems also increase in size as they move upward. Because of the enormous change and high increase in complexity, the yellow level (7, G-T or A'-N') had to be depicted as large as all previous levels combined.

In another illustration, overlapping emerging and subsiding wave-like lines show that there are always several levels active at the same time. The x-axis depicts the temporal span of the appearance of external existential problems. The y-axis depicts the respective activation of the individual coping systems.

In Graves' "Summary Statement", all key points of his theory converge and show his work as a whole.

OUTLOOK

First of all, we want to thank you that you've taken the time to take a deeper look at the work of Clare W. Graves. We believe it can actually help understand and potentially solve some of our time's most pressing issues and conflicts. Being able to apply the different levels of existence to national and international political topics, global issues concerning the economy, environment and cultural differences, can be a first step to better understand the underlying values, ways of thinking and deriving behaviors, to then facilitate and accelerate resolutions as well as positive change.

We also want to encourage you to integrate these learnings in your daily lives. You might start seeing these levels / colors everywhere: at home, at work, on TV, in political elections, in advertising - to just name a few.

Take another look at yourself and your immediate and greater environment. What are your most important values? What motivates you? What annoys you? What makes you happy? Are there recurring issues or conflicts you keep running into at work or in relationships? Who did you vote for and why? How do like to be managed and how do you manage others? What's the corporate culture at your workplace like? How are business decisions being made? What does your country's government stand for? What policies are they trying to implement and how does that reflect on the party's and its leaders' value systems? How are different nations trying to solve complex geopolitical and environmental problems?

Through his many years of research, Graves developed a valuable, complex theory, which can facilitate the understanding and explanation of many aspects of this world. Or in the words of journalist Nicholas Steed: "The theory that explains everything".

Awareness is the first step of the journey. We invite you to start it now.

ABOUT THE AUTHORS

RAINER KRUMM

Rainer Krumm is a managerial trainer, consultant and coach. He studied business education and strategic management and has guided, advised, trained and coached international entrepreneurs, top executives and teams in more than 23 countries. He is one of the most experienced international consultants and trainers in the area of corporate culture and change management.

For over ten years, he has worked with Gravesian theory in managerial consultation. He was trained by Chris Cowan in SPIRAL DYNAMICS®. Together with Martina Bär and Hartmut Wiehle, he wrote the first

German-language book on Gravesian theory which was published under the title "Unternehmen verstehen, gestalten, verändern – Das Graves-Value-System in der Praxis" (Understanding, shaping and changing enterprises – the Graves value system in practice) in 2007. His book "9 Levels of Value Systems" has been published in both German and English. For managers, he wrote the book "30 Minuten für werteorientiertes Führen" (Thirty minutes for value-oriented leadership), which brings Gravesian theory into focus for leadership.

BENEDIKT PARSTORFER

Benedikt Parstorfer is a learning and development trainer, passionate educator and avid public speaker, based in New York City. He holds a graduate degree in organizational psychology and group dynamics and is a certified NLP Trainer. Together with co-author Rainer Krumm, he built and further developed assessment tools based on the Graves model and certified over 120 coaches, consultants and trainers in the tools' application. Originally introduced to Graves' ECLET model during his NLP Trainer certification in Vienna in 2012, he has since then become an expert in and advocate of Graves' work.

Contact the authors:

www.9levels.com

www.benediktparstorfer.com

BIBLIOGRAPHY

GRAVES' WORKS – BOOKS, ARTICLES, AND LECTURES

Graves, C.W.: Individual differences in irritability in the male rat. Master of Arts Thesis, Western Reserve University, Hudson, 1943

Graves, C.W.: A study of the genesis and dynamics of psychopathic personality as revealed by combining the clinical case history and experimental approaches. Doctoral Thesis, Western Reserve University, Hudson, 1945

Graves, C. W.: The Implications to Management of System – Ethical Theory. S.l., 1962

Graves, C. W.: Value System And Their Relation to Managerial Controls And Organizational Viability. Schenectady, 1965

Graves, C. W., Huntley, W. C., LaBier, D. W.: Personality Structure and Perceptual Readiness; An Investigation of Their Relationship to Hypothesized Levels of Human Existence. Schenectady, 1965

Graves, C. W.: Deterioration of Work Standards. Harvard Business Review, 44(5), 1966, pp. 117–128

Graves, C. W.: Levels of Existence: An Open System Theory of Values. Journal of Humanistic Psychology, Alameda, 10(2), 1970, pp. 131–155

Graves, C. W., Madden H.T.; Madden, L.P.: The Congruent Management Strategy. S.l. 1970

Graves, C. W.: How Should Who Lead Whom to do What? YMCA Management Forum, Schenectady, 1971–1972

Graves, C. W.: Human Nature Prepares for a Momentous Leap. The Futurist, No. 8, Bethesda, 1974, pp. 72–87

Graves, C. W., Summary Statement: The Emergent, Cyclical, Double-Helix Model of Adult Human Biopsychosocial Systems. Boston, 1981

Graves, C. W.: Levels of Human Existence. Ed. Lee, W.R. Santa Barbara, ECLET, 2002

Graves, C. W.: The Never Ending Quest. Eds. Cowan, C.C., Todorovic N. Santa Barbara, ECLET, 2005

Lee, B.: Transcription of a "Seminar on Levels of Human Existence" conducted by Dr Graves at the Washington School of Psychiatry. Washington, 16 October1971

ADDITIONAL LITERATURE

Bär, M., Krumm, R., Wiehle, H.: Unternehmen verstehen, gestalten verändern – Das Graves-Value-System in der Praxis.. Gabler Verlag, Wiesbaden, 2nd expanded edition, 2007

Beck, D. E., Cowan, C. C.: Spiral Dynamics – Mastering Values, Leadership and Change. Blackwell Publishing, Williston 1996

Beck, D., Larsen, T.H.; Solonin, S., Viljoen, R, Johns, T., Spiral Dynamics in Action: Humanity's Master Code; Wiley, Hoboken, 2018

Caspers S, Heim S, Lucas MG, Stephan E, Fischer L, et al.: Dissociated Neural Processing for Decisions in Managers and Non-Managers. PLoS ONE 7(8): e43537. doi:10.1371/journal.pone.0043537, 2012

Krumm, R.: 9 Levels of Value Systems. Werdewelt Verlags- und Medienhaus, Haiger, 2012

Krumm, R.: 30 Minuten für werteorientiertes Führen, Gabal Verlag, Offenbach, 2014

Tad, J.; Woodsmall, W.: Time Line. Junfermann Verlag, Paderborn, 1991

FILM DOCUMENTS

Cliff Macintosh interviews Clare W. Graves. NYC Consulting & ECLET Publishing, Santa Barbara, 2005

In Conversation with Dr. Clare W. Graves. NYC Consulting & ECLET Publishing, Santa Barbara, 2005

AUDIO DOCUMENTS

Beck, D.: Spiral Dynamics Integral. Sounds True, Boulder, 2006

INTERNET SOURCES

www.clarewgraves.com

LIST OF SOURCES FOR FIGURES

Title: Courtesy of Special Collections, Schaffer Library, Union College

Figure 1: Courtesy of Special Collections, Schaffer Library, Union College

Figure 2: Wikipedia Commons (http://en.wikipedia.org/wiki/File:Unionaerial2.jpg)

Figure 3 self-created

Figure 4: Master's thesis of Clare W. Graves, 1943

Figure 5, above and below: Annual Commencement Convocation, Western Reserve University, 1943

Figure 6: Doctoral thesis of Clare W. Graves, 1945

Figures 7, 8, 9, 10, 11, 12, 13, 14, and 15: self-created, based on the data from "Let the data talk" in Lee, W.R.: Levels of Human Existence, 2005

Figures 16 and 19 self-created, based on the original graphic in Lee, W.R.: Levels of Human Existence, 2005

Figure 20: self-created, based on original graphic in Graves, C.W.: Deterioration of Work Standards, 1966

Figures 21 and 22: self-created, based on original graphic in Graves, C.W.: How Should Who Lead Whom To Do What?, 1971–72

Figures 23, 24, and 25: self-created, based on original graphics from Graves, C.W.: Summary Statement, 1981

GABAL global
English Editions by GABAL Publishing

Who We Are

GABAL provides proven practical knowledge and publishes media products on the topics of business, success, and life. With over 600 experienced, international authors from various industries and education, we inspire businesses and people to move forward.

GABAL. Your publisher.
Motivating. Sympathetic. Pragmatic.

These three adjectives describe the core brand of GABAL. They describe how we think, feel, and work. They describe the style and mission of our books and media. GABAL is your publisher, because we want to bring you forward. Not with finger-pointing, not divorced from reality, not pointy-headed or purely academic, but motivating in effect, sympathetic in appearance, and pragmatically-oriented toward results.

Our books have only one concern: they want to help the reader improve. In business. For success. In life.

Our target reader
People who want to develop personally and/or professionally

As a modern media house GABAL publishes books, audio books, and e-books for people and companies that want to develop further. Our books are aimed at people who are looking for knowledge about current issues in business and education that can be put into practice quickly.

For more information, see the GABAL global website:

http://www.iuniverse.com/Packages/GABAL-Global-Editions.aspx

CPSIA information can be obtained
at www.ICGtesting.com
Printed in the USA
LVHW09s1419300818
588655LV00001B/95/P